The Mediating Effect of Public Opinion on Public Policy

SUNY series in Public Policy
Anne Schneider and Helen Ingram, editors

The Mediating Effect of Public Opinion on Public Policy

Exploring the Realm of Health Care

RICHARD E. CHARD

STATE UNIVERSITY OF NEW YORK PRESS

Published by
State University of New York

© 2004 State University of New York

For information, address State University of New York Press,
90 State Street, Suite 700, Albany, NY 12207

Production by Michael Haggett
Marketing by Jennifer Giovani and Susan M. Petrie

Library of Congress Cataloging-in-Publication Data

Chard, Richard E., 1965–
    The mediating effect of public opinion on public policy : exploring the realm of health care /
Richard E. Chard.
        p. cm. — (SUNY series in public policy)
    Includes bibliographical references and index.
    ISBN 0-7914-6053-3 (hbk. : alk. paper) — ISBN 0-7914-6054-1 (pbk. : alk. paper)
        1. Medical care—Public opinion. 2. Medical policy—public opinion. 3. Health
planning—Public opinion. 4. Public opinion. I. Title. II. Series.

RA395.A3C4795 2004
362.1—dc22

                                                                                    2003070438

10 9 8 7 6 5 4 3 2 1

For Cristina

Contents

Acknowledgments

My thanks and gratitude to Paul Teske, Mark Schneider and Jeff Segal for their help and support

Chapter 1

Health Policy Change

An Attitudinal Approach

WHY HAS HEALTH CARE DOMINATED THE POLICY AGENDA?

In 1990, Helen Jones, a single mother of two, learned that she had diabetes. Anyone in the medical profession could have told her that she was at high risk, after all, she was of Native American heritage, and she was somewhat overweight. Helen's physician told her that her condition was manageable and that her yearly visits to the doctor must now become more frequent. Helen's job at a local factory came with excellent benefits, and although she was concerned about her illness, she knew that as long as she followed her doctor's advice, it was not life threatening.

Helen's life changed dramatically the following year when the factory closed. Not only was Helen out of work, in a recession-ridden economy, she was also faced with the prospect of losing her health insurance. While her unemployment benefits insured that she and her children would not starve, they were not nearly enough to cover her COBRA payments of $400 per month. When Helen did find a new job, she learned that her preexisting condition prohibited her from obtaining health insurance under her new employer's plan. Suddenly, health care and health insurance had gone from a trivial consideration to a highly salient one.

One night while watching the news, Helen saw a political advertisement for Harris Wofford, a Senate candidate. In the ad Wofford talked about health care coverage as a national issue. For Helen, and many other citizens throughout the United States, this message resonated. The ad, and Wofford's campaign, were

1

the product of James Carville and Paul Begalia. Together, they were responsible for turning a special election to fill the remaining years of Senator John Heinz's seat from a sleepy contest, in which a popular former governor and Bush administration attorney general, Richard Thornburgh, would win, into a galvanizing event for the public provision of health care as a political issue. The Wofford victory on May 8, 1991, was probably not surprising to those who had been watching Gallup's "Most Important Issue Surveys." As Table 1.1 and the accompanying graph (Figure 1.1) show, health care became increasingly important. In fact, by 1992, health care surpassed crime, the deficit, and drugs as the most important problem facing the United States in Gallup surveys.

In 1992, following on the heels of Harris Wofford's stunning upset victory in Pennsylvania, then Governor Bill Clinton hired Wofford's advisers to help him run his dark-horse presidential campaign. Paul Begala and James Carville

TABLE 1.1
Gallup's Most Important Issues Surveys: 1980–2000

Year	Crime	Health Care	Deficit	Drugs
1980	2	0	0	1
1981	5	0	0	0
1982	4	0	0	0
1983	2	0	0	0
1984	4	0	5	2
1985	0	5	4	—
1986	3	0	11	0
1987	3	1	11	10
1988	3	1	4	2
1989	4	0	6	39
1990	1	0	21	18
1991	5	5	5	12
1992	7	10	7	8
1993	13	23	14	6
1994	42	25	5	8
1995	26	10	13	8
1996	23	9	18	9
1997	20	7	6	15
1998	15	6	4	11
1999	15	6	2	6
2000	11	10	1	6

Note: Numbers are percentages of respondents indicating that the category is the most important issue.

FIGURE 1.1
Gallup's Most Important Issues Surveys: 1980–2000

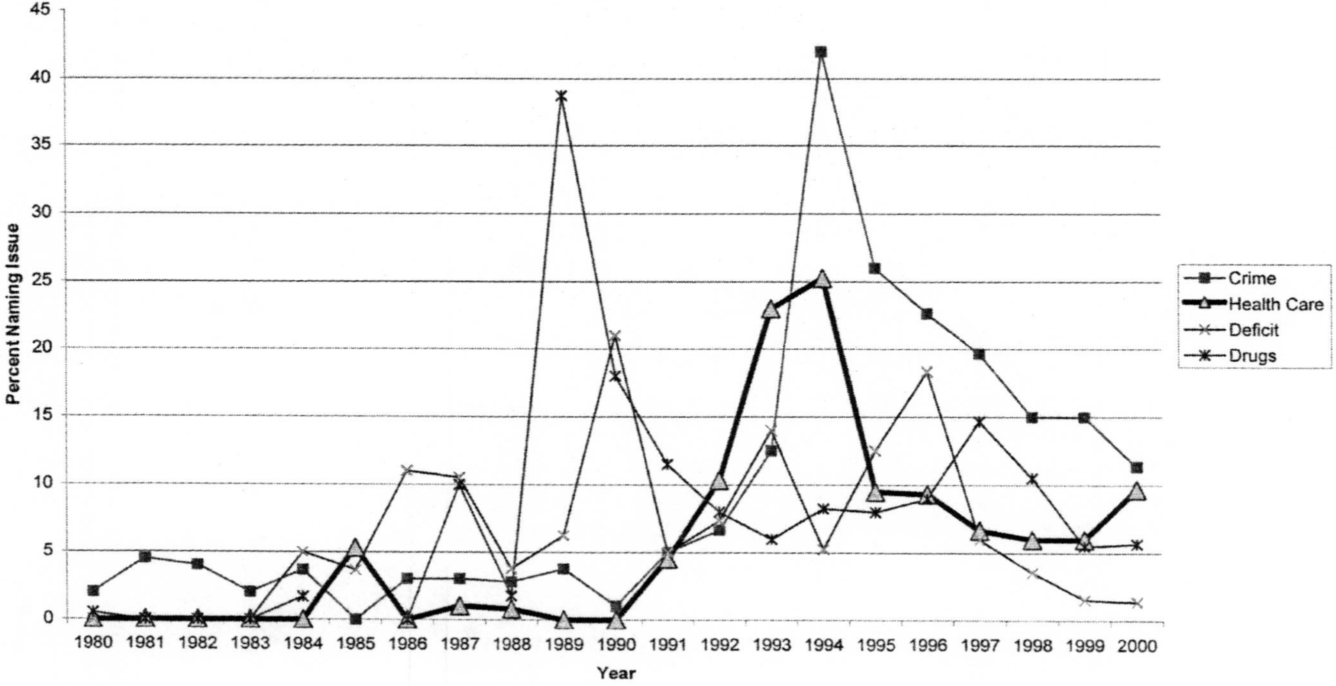

took the health care message that had resonated so well in Pennsylvania to the "Little Rock War Room" and the rest is, as they say, history. The election of 1992 and the subsequent introduction of the Clinton administration's Health Security Act in 1993 are the most recent entries in the modern history of health care reform. In fact, much of this book is dedicated to a series of analyses of the Health Security Act because it *is* among the most recent entries in the modern history of health care provision; however, the story itself began in 1933. During the seven decades since then, the debate has centered on what role government can and should play. This is a debate that has been shaped and influenced by politicians, political elites, the media, and the general population.

EXPLANATIONS FROM SOCIAL SCIENCE

The question now is what can the social sciences tell us about the events of the past 68 years? Can the social sciences tell us why the United States is the only Western democracy without government-provided health care? Is the health insurance system in the United States a product of politics, economics, or both? Most important, can social sciences tell us what role citizens and politicians have played in this remarkable journey?

In this book, the reciprocal relationship between voters and politicians is examined within the context of knowledge. To that end, I explore how advocacy efforts affect the dominant ideology by informing and persuading the public to support or oppose health care policy changes and proposals. The study is multifaceted because of the complexity of the relationships and the desire to discover what comprises the turbulence beneath the system that leads to the observable dynamic changes in policy. Further, there is also a focus on understanding why policy proposals fail, which is again, as I show in the remaining chapters, also a function of the underlying activity. For example, in chapter four, I examine the role of the president as an advocate in a unidirectional model with the president as the first actor in health policy change. Rather than looking at the role of various political factors as predecessors to presidential action, this study considers the simultaneous effect of politics on presidential advocacy in health care policy. That is not to say that the president acts in a vacuum, something that Cameron (2000) demonstrates convincingly. Rather, I construct a multistage cross-sectional pooled time series model of presidential decision making that takes into account measurable components of the political context within which the president makes a health care policy proposal. This is one example of my attempt throughout this book to simplify relationships that are complex and present snapshots that will add to our understanding of how policy develops within an environment where the information held by the political actors (politicians and voters) is dynamic.

Building on that concept, I examine how the dynamic nature of knowledge affects policy preferences. This raises the question How can a researcher uncover and disentangle this relationship? Without giving away the story, the short answer is that knowledge and policy preferences and the reciprocal relationship they share is observable by means of studying public opinion. In this sense, the responses to survey questions represent the underlying process in which information and preferences are in a constant state of flux. For example, a citizen's knowledge on policy issues can change through exposure to a number of different sources ranging from political elites to the media. The aggregate effect of these changes can create sways in public opinion about policy preferences. These changes in public policy preferences then provide politicians and elites with additional information that allows them to change their message, which in turn can again affect information held by the general public. In a nutshell, this is the cycle of activity that leads to the dynamic changes in policy that advance in a discontinuous manner within a path dependent system. The examination of this cycle of policy stability, punctuated equilibriums and the underlying turbulence in various forms and various stages, is a central element of this book.

The study of this cycle is necessarily grounded in a study of public opinion in its various forms, which leads first to a discussion of whether there is an influence of public opinion on national policy. The question of whether public opinion influences national policy is an area of debate. Some deny any influence, while others suggest that the causal arrow is in the opposite direction with public policy influencing public opinion. In the following chapters, I examine this relationship to learn whether public preferences have any influence over policy outcomes. I also examine the influence of advocacy and information on public preferences. Public opinion is a chief example of the underlying turbulence that exists. It becomes more relevant when opportunities for punctuated equilibria appear, but it is nevertheless generally at a level that is just beneath the surface and not always identifiable. Jacobs and Shapiro (2000) give excellent examples of this underlying dynamic where elites believe that public opinion can be shaped and influenced by advocacy and information. Likewise, they show that politicians rely on public opinion to craft their messages. While more specific examples presented in *Politicians Don't Pander* are discussed in the following chapters of this book, Jacobs and Shapiro provide a nice example of the overall concept in their introduction made even more salient by their use of recent political events:

> Republicans' dogged pursuit of impeachment was premised on the assumption that poll honed presentations would ultimately win public support for their actions. We suggest that this kind of overconfidence in the power of crafted talk to move public opinion explains the political overreaching and failure that was vividly displayed by Clinton's

health reform effort during the 1993–94 period and the Republicans' campaign for their policy objectives beginning with their "Contract with America" during 1995–96. Crafted talk has been more effective in opposing rather than promoting policy initiatives partly because the news media represent and magnify disagreement but also because politicians' overconfidence in crafted talk has prompted them to promote policy goals that do not enjoy the support of most Americans or moderate legislators. (p. xv)

Despite the fact that this is a brief introduction to their argument, in general, Jacobs and Shapiro show that among politicians there is a belief that public opinion can be used as a source of information about the construction of policy proposals (e.g., the Health Security Act) as well as a belief that public opinion can be changed through the use of crafted talk (e.g., the Clinton impeachment process). This notion fits well within the Downsian (1957) concept of democracy in which political elites search for information regarding preferred policies among the citizens (polls) and citizens search for information from elites about which policies they should favor (crafted talk). (This concept will be discussed further in chapter 2.) However, as Jacobs and Shapiro suggest, something goes terribly awry in that crafted talk often results in an irrational turn of events causing a disconnect between policies preferred by citizens and policies preferred by politicians.

Nevertheless, by applying our understanding of the discontinuous events, known as "punctuated equilibria" when discussed within the context of path dependence, the relationship begins to make more sense and does, in fact, fit within a rational paradigm. If the goal of crafted talk, or advocacy and information directed toward the public by the elites, is to create conditions that are ripe for a dynamic change in policy, then crafted talk is imminently rational for politicians. Likewise, if the goal among elites in consulting public opinion is to determine whether there is disequilibria in the policy system due to dissatisfaction among the public, then the use of polls is again rational elite behavior. The breakdown occurs when there are strong policy preferences among the citizens that are in direct conflict with the strong policy preferences of elites. In such a situation, there can be no rational outcome. Thus, it is crucial to understand that public policy and public opinion do not operate in a vacuum. While they influence and inform each other, there are a multitude of additional factors that influence both public policy and public opinion. In this book, these other factors—advocacy efforts, the political climate, the public mood, the media, and various forms of information—are discussed within the context of the relationship between public opinion and public policy. Together, they produce a better understanding of the underlying unrest that occasionally allows American health care policy to leap from one path dependent equilibrium to another.

Of course, this argument rests on the assumption that public opinion in some way, shape, or form influences public policy.

OVERVIEW

Indeed, this requirement was met, time and time again, in many cases by the president. In chapter 4, I show that during the modern era of politics (1933 to the present) there have been multiple attempts, led by the presidents, to institute a national health insurance plan. Beginning with the first draft of Social Security legislation and continuing through the 1960s, there were frequent proposals; however, it was not until 1965 with the passage of Medicare and Medicaid that the federal and state governments became providers of comprehensive health benefits packages for civilians.[1]

Each of the following chapters focuses on a specific element of the seemingly random shocks to the path dependent system or the punctuated equilibria in the dynamic system. In chapter 2, I put forth a theoretical framework for studying dynamic policy change. The discussion thus far has alluded to path dependence, punctuated equilibria, and the role that the political actors play within the system of dynamic policy change. These examinations are used to gain greater understanding of the nature of health care policy change, in general, and the role that the mediating effect of the public or the instigating effect of politicians play in these events. The system is indeed complex, as Lippmann (1965) noted many deacades ago:

> The real environment is altogether too big, too complex and too fleeting for direct acquaintance. We are not equipped to deal with so much subtlety, so much variety, so many permutations and combinations. And although we have to act in that environment, we have to reconstruct it on a simpler model before we can manage with it. (p. 11)

For the very reason that Lippman notes, in the chapters that follow, the various parts of the underlying turbulence that presents policymakers with opportunities for evolutionary policy changes are broken down into smaller components. This deconstruction begins in chapter 3 where the exploration of path dependence in policy begins with an examination of two variables that nicely model path dependence, public mood and federal spending. Federal spending can be viewed as a path dependent system by the very fact that each year's budget builds on the budget of the previous year. The public mood presents an insight into the evolutionary changes that transform policy. By examining the mediating effect of public opinion on federal health care expenditures in chapter 3, I examine one feature of the turbulence that leads to evolutionary policy change. In contrast to the other chapters, where the role of public opinion and political instigation are examined simultaneously, in chapter 3, public mood is isolated as one component of the underlying unrest. I investigate how the public and their mood have mediated federal health care policy by performing a time series analysis. Specifically, chapter 3 demonstrates the mediating and predictive impact of public mood on federal health care expenditures. In sum, as the public becomes more liberal in its attitudes, federal health care spending increases. This finding also provides insight into the failure of the Health Security Act. While the public had become more liberal in the decade leading up to the Act, it had not become liberal enough to support the Act's required expenditures. Thus, chapter 3 puts forth one simple explanation for the failure of the Act and the success of Medicare and Medicaid.

In chapter 4, I begin exploring some of the other components of the underlying turbulence. Specifically, I examine the instigating role of politicians. In this case, the president is viewed in terms of being the chief instigator, and the discussion takes place on the backdrop of the modern history of federal health care policy. This chapter focuses on the actions and activities of the president and the context in which they are made from the perspective of what Jacobs and Shapiro (2000) call "crafted talk." I present an examination of how presidential speeches and other presidential discussions of health care have combined with traditional notions of presidential power to shape the debate and the ultimate outcomes of presidential health policy initiatives. Overall, three presidents—Harry Truman, Lyndon Johnson, and Bill Clinton—actively pursued national health care reform with varying degrees of success. Their ability to achieve dynamic health policy change was tempered by the political environment in which they operated. At times, factors exogenous to the policy area itself established situations in which only incremental change was possible. Generally, the politician influences the situation through one of two roles: either as an active participant shaping the policy outputs so that the public gets what it wants or as a bystander watching policy advance incrementally. That is, without effort, change can only occur through evolution, but with active politicians acting as policy entrepreneurs, change can be dynamic. Of course, this can be tempered or accelerated by citizens. The role of the public, their mood and their preferences, influence the nature of the policy change.

The first part of the book (chapters 3 and 4) investigates the mediating effects of public opinion and elite instigation across most of the modern political era. Together, they provide a base for an in-depth exploration of what many have called the most sweeping policy proposal of the past decade, the Health Security Act. The latter part of the book (chapters 5, 6, and 7) explores the demise of the Act in more depth, with an emphasis on uncovering the underlying dynamic that leads to evolutionary changes in policy. To that end, chapter 5 examines the role of policy specific knowledge on citizen support for a policy. In this case, an investigation of how factual knowledge of the Health Security Act affected public support for it is presented. Generally, the finding is that people more knowledgeable about the details of the Act were much more likely to support it. This is an important finding, given that the general consensus was that the Act failed, not because it was contrary to what the public wanted, but rather because it was so complex that most people did not realize it was the plan they had wanted. Thus, in this case, the evolutionary path was blocked by complexity. The Clinton administration was unable to maintain public support or persuade the undecided partly because of the complexity of his plan and also due to the simplicity of the countervailing message. The public and politicians alike were forced to abandon the Health Security Act because Clinton's crafted talk was not completely comprehensible.

The role and power of information, a factor that proves to be crucial to policy support in the analysis presented in chapter 5, is explored further in chapter 6. However, in chapter 6, the media is brought into the discussion through an examination of the "Harry and Louise" advertising campaign's influence on support for the Health Security Act. There is a significant impact from the countervalent information that is seen in diminished support among those exposed to the advertisements. This chapter represents the final analysis of the underlying turbulence in the health care policy system. Together, chapters 3, 4, 5, and 6 explore (within the context of public opinion and elite discourse) the conditions under which policy can change, and why, even when the conditions are right, policy does not change.

With chapter 7, the investigation of public opinion and elite discourse comes full circle. That is, while in chapter 4, I discuss the role of the president, his power, and popularity in pursuing policy change, in chapter 7, I examine how negative campaigns against presidential policies affect vote intentions, by scrutinizing the effect of the Harry and Louise advertising campaign on intentions to vote for Bill Clinton. The impact in chapter 7 is much more dramatic than the findings in chapter 6. Exposure to the Harry and Louise advertisements significantly decreased the likelihood of voting for Clinton in 1996. Further, these results point to a plausible explanation for the 1994 elections in which the Democrats suffered the most stunning loss in their history, losing both houses of Congress by margins larger than any incumbent party in history, because of the lingering negative attitudes toward the Clinton administration. While chapter 7 deals with a concept that is not directly related to the discussion of path dependence in the preceding chapters, it provides data and findings to enhance our understanding of the nature of policy change. These results show that there can be a downside to tapping into the turbulent undercurrents that allow policy changes from time to time.

Overall, this book explores the small, but significant, impact that citizen preferences play in federal health care policy. The following chapters present examinations of areas where public opinion is influenced at the margins, advocacy by the president, attitudes toward spending, information, and political sophistication. Taken together, they show that, although public opinion does not dictate public policy, there are indeed mediating influences on policy from various aspects of public opinion.

Chapter 2

Exploring the Foundations of
Dynamic Policy Change

PATH DEPENDENCE

In the previous chapter, I put forth a series of broad questions regarding what social sciences can do to explain how health care policy has developed over the past 68 years. The answers to these questions necessarily begin with an exploration of the theories available in the social sciences to explain the phenomenon.

One important theory that may help answer these questions is path dependence (North, 1990; Wilsford, 1994). This is a plausible explanation because throughout the history of medicine, there has clearly been some political connection. From the development of the first institutions to the present, politics and health have been intertwined. Thus, it is logical that political economists' notions of path dependence—a system in which all present norms, policies, and institutions—exist because of a series of past choices that dictate the direction of future policies, norms, and institutions, would provide a theoretical framework (North, 1990; Wilsford, 1994). The question at this point is whether the theory of path dependence can explain why the United States is the last Western democracy to rely on markets to supply health care to its citizens. The examination of why this is so is the focus of this work. It is an interesting story that touches on all levels of politics in that there is a role for each political actor, from the president to the general public, all of whom have played a role in the development of the current state of health care. In this book, I present studies of how the actions and activities of these individuals have contributed to the debate over the formulation of health care policy. Oftentimes, it is a story of power, but in many of the most interesting cases, it is the story of the power of knowledge. To understand why the United States is the only

11

Western democracy without universal health care, we must first explore the rationale for Americans' confidence in markets to supply health care.

As I mentioned earlier, one possible explanation for the reliance on markets is grounded in a discussion of path dependence. Wilsford (1994) describes that "a path-dependent sequence of political changes is one that is tied to previous decisions and existing institutions" (p. 252), which, as North (1990) adds leads to a system of incremental change. This view has some support when one observes the political changes in the provision and financing of health care in the United States over the past seventy years. For example, even the most sweeping changes, such as Medicare, stem from incremental changes to existing institutions such as Social Security. Indeed, Medicare was appended to Social Security, likewise, Medicaid was appended to Medicare and most recently, the State Childrens' Health Insurance Program (SCHIP) was appended to Medicaid. Wilsford (1994) defines this as "low politics," which relies on existing institutional structures to "channel present and future policy along certain paths" (p. 256).

One question that is central to a path dependent discussion of the politics of health care provision is whether health care is a privilege or a right. The idea that health care is a right derives from collectivist societies; that is, societies that believe that each person needs to contribute to society and that in order to contribute a person must be healthy. In fact, as Viscusi and Evans (1990) note, health status affects not only the performance of work, but also the utility derived from work. Thus, good health is a necessity for a productive society. Further, preventive health has benefits for the population, such as reduced risk of disease and epidemics, and consequently it is in the best interests of the state to promote healthiness. The path dependent adherents argue that the way in which each country promotes health is dictated by the political culture of the country. For example, in the United States, where, since its founding, minimal government has been viewed as the ideal, one would expect the governmental role in health care to also be minimal. In contrast, in a country like Great Britain, which was one of the first to adopt a social security pension plan, one would expect a much more active role to be played by government in the provision of health care. These expectations are born out by the facts. Great Britain has national health insurance, even through times of conservative government, while the United States has never embraced the idea of universal health care, even during the most liberal governments (Jacobs, 1993).

In the United States, federal intervention in health care is consistently constrained and incremental. Generally, major health care reform movements in the United States are the product of forceful advocacy by the president, aligned with like-minded groups to create entrepreneurial movements. However, only when societal conditions permitted deviations from the notion that health care is a private good have these movements succeeded.

Thus, it is clear that the central question is whether health care is a privilege or a right. The answer to that question can go far in helping us understand whether health policy in the United States is determined due to path dependence or whether there is some other explanation. Unlike other commodities, health care cannot be easily defined in the traditional sense as a public good or as a private good. Instead, the definition of health care depends on the individual—in other words, how one views health care politically is a function of individual attitudes. Therefore, health care policy, unlike many other areas of public policy, is grounded in and constrained by the aggregated preferences of citizens. The belief that health care is a privilege or, in contrast, a right is based more on individual preference than on an overall understanding of the policy issues.

For instance, consider a policy area such as defense, the environment, or education. Now try to imagine arguments that any one of these should be solely a private good. That is, try to imagine a credible argument that citizens should buy as much defense as they want, or as much clean air as they need, or as much K–12 education as they desire. While all of these policy areas have supplemental private good components (e.g., citizens can buy guns or air purifiers or go to private schools), they are in addition to an existing level of goods and services publicly provided.

This is not so with health care in the United States because while the debate over whether defense, the environment, or education is a public or private good was settled long ago, the war over the nature of health care is still raging. This battle is not focused on how health care policy and the means to obtain access to health care can be arranged in a typology of public and private goods, rather, the debate is fueled by individual attitudes and ideologies. Thus, the market for health care provision is truly in the eye of the beholder. Whether one views health care as a commodity that we should publicly finance is driven by one's ideology. However, as I show in this book, the dominant ideology can be shaped and molded through advocacy and information. This is fitting with the notion of path dependence, in that the theory allows for "discontinuous change [with] features in common with discontinuous evolutionary change (characterized in demographic theory as punctuated equilibrium), but perhaps its most striking feature is that it is seldom as discontinuous as it appears on the surface" (North, 1990, p. 90). The notion of punctuated equilibrium has been embraced as a means to study rapid policy change that cannot be justified through traditional reliance on theories of incremental change (Baumgartner & Jones, 1993; Schneider & Teske with Mintrom 1995). Thus, one way to study health policy and health policy change is within this notion of path dependence wherein there is a possibility for dynamic, rather than incremental, change. That would explain why the United States has some components of national health care (Medicare and to a lesser extent Medicaid and SCHIP) and why, at times, politicians have explored other options although never adopted them (the Health Security Act and Catastrophic Care). If this is the case, then the question of why the United States is the only Western democracy without national health care is really a question of what keeps the system in equilibrium as a market model for the provision of health care. Further, how can we explain the instances when there have been such disequilibria that major revisions to health care policy have gone from the back burner to the national agenda?

As Baumgartner and Jones (1993) note, there must be some instability in the equilibrium to get to a point where the issue of disequilibria will capture the attention of policymakers. However, they argue that there is always a stabilizing effect that arises from policy subsystems, norms, and institutions, what I collectively refer to as the "dominant ideology." Thus, even where there is some disequilibria, policy cannot and will not change in a vacuum. This is the very same point that North (1990) made in writing that the discontinuity observed on the surface in a case of punctuated equilibrium is actually the result of a turbulent mix beneath the surface. One possible explanation is that the turbulence beneath the surface and the resulting change in the dominant ideology is due to advocacy and information.

Advocacy and information are necessarily intertwined in a reciprocal relationship. In the classical model (Downs 1957) of policy preferences, simplicity is the goal. As a result, knowledge is imputed to all participants and voters, platforms and candidates are driven to a point of convergence, the median. However, as positive political theorists tell us (see Hinich & Munger, 1997, for example), the study of policy preferences is more complicated in the real world. These new models take into account uncertainty about the preferences of candidates and voters. Uncertainty, in its simplest form, is the lack of knowledge. Thus, while the classical model assumes that everyone in the political system has full information, the successors assume that there is a degree of uncertainty associated with that knowledge.

THE IMPORTANCE OF PUBLIC OPINION IN SHAPING HEALTH CARE POLICY

Generally speaking, the idea that public opinion can and does influence public policy is not new. If we understand public opinion to be the general preferences of the people and we accept that the U.S. government is based on the premise that the public makes their preferences known at regular intervals through elections and referenda (Kingdon, 1984), we can then draw the conclusion that public opinion influences the U.S. government through the traditional democratic process. The notion that public preference can be conveyed through forms other than elections, such as grassroots efforts and public advocacy groups, is more novel. The idea that policy is dictated by public opinion through survey polls is revolutionary.

Page and Shapiro (1992) argue that the idea of policy determined by popular will is a positive component of American democracy. The authors state, in contrast to the Madisonian concept of democracy, "that ordinary citizens are not to be feared, that governments should respond to their wishes, and that the politically active should learn more about what the public wants" (ix). Throughout their work, the authors demonstrate their conviction that direct democracy can be achieved by listening to the various ways in which the public expresses itself, and that popular and successful policies rise up from the public rather than being imposed on the public.

Overall, Page and Shapiro demonstrate that there is both "rhyme and reason" to the preferences of the American public. They argue that the public is rational in its preferences and that these preferences represent attitudes that do not vacillate wildy, but instead advance and evolve over time. The authors write:

> [T]he collective policy preferences of the American public are predominately *rational*, in the sense that they are *real*—not meaningless, random "nonattitudes"; that they are generally *stable*, seldom changing by large amounts and rarely fluctuating back and forth; that they form *coherent* and mutually consistent (not self-contradictory) patterns, involving meaningful distinctions; that these patterns *make sense* in terms of underlying values and available information; that, when collective policy preferences change, they almost always do so in *understandable* and, indeed, *predictable* ways, reacting in consistent fashion to international events and social and economic changes as reported by the mass media; and finally, that opinion changes generally constitute *sensible* adjustments to new conditions and new information that are communicated to the public. (1992: lxx).

The intent of this book is to demonstrate that public opinion is indeed rational and coherent, given the information available. Focusing on health care as a policy area, numerous examples are presented to demonstrate that policy is influenced by the attitudes of the public and the elites. Specifically, these discussions show that health care policy advances in concert with public attitudes, and that these changes in health care policy do in fact make sense given the public's underlying values and the information available to them. In short, the argument here is that the path of health care policy is in fact predictable when one understands the influence of public opinion, and prior health care policy itself. To understand how this occurs, it is first necessary to understand where health care policy is presently, and how it evolved into its current state.

AMERICAN HEALTH CARE POLICY

Health care policy has been public policy since the founding of the United States. The first federal foray into health care was the beginning of an incrementalist and path dependent system that continues to the present. In 1798, President John Adams established the Marine Hospital Service to care for sick and disabled seamen (National Institutes of Health [NIH], 2001). In spite of this, federal intervention in health care remained minimal—with most regulation and public health initiatives occurring at the state level. However, in 1902 more than 100 years after its founding, during a time when the health care problems faced by the United States became more complex, in true incrementalist fashion, the Marine Hospital Service evolved into the Public Health and Marine Hospital Service and added a new entity, the Hygienic Laboratory to oversea Public Law 244, which was designed to "regulate the shipment of biologics" (NIH, 2001). By 1912, the Public Health and Marine Hospital Service had become simply the Public Health Service, and in 1930, the Hygienic Laboratory became the National Institutes of Health. Under the direction of President Franklin Roosevelt, the NIH grew to encompass a wide variety of public health policies and issues, and under Title VI of the Social Security Act, the NIH was given the authority to administer $2 million in grants to the states for health care initiatives (NIH, 2001). According to Charles Schottland, the first director of the Social Security Administration, the grants to the states were a strategic move by the president. Roosevelt was looking for a way to establish a national institution to study all aspects of health in the United States. Having been thwarted by the Congress and the Supreme Court, he sought to base this "new" institution in an existing law. His aides discovered that the revisions to the 1798 law enabling the government to provide health care for veterans of the Navy also enabled Roosevelt to establish, through bureaucratic rather than legislative means, an enduring health care institution that may some day evolve into the kind of national health system envisioned by his secretary of labor, Frances Perkins. Of course, between 1798 and 1937, there was other public involvement in health care, but it was limited to regulation and small-scale, publicly funded health care for Native Americans and military personnel. This demonstrates the slow nature of change in health care policy in the United States from 1789 to the 1930s. If the path dependent framework is correct, this slowly changing foundation is the structure upon which all subsequent national health care policies rest. Further, it would be safe to assume that the turbulence that North (1990) associates with periods of change in path dependent systems was in fact surprisingly calm. Thus, one would expect that health care policy at the federal level would be slow to change and when change did occur, it would be built around existing institutions, following the evolutionary path of the Public Health Service and the National Institutes of Health.

However, something changed during the 1930s. Health care became a more prominent issue. This was true in part because the nature of health care was changing, private health insurers had entered the picture (Feldstein, 1993), and in the United Kingdom, the closest ally of the United States, the National Health Service was founded. Thus, by the 1930s, the private market nature of the doctor-patient relationship was changed by health insurance and in addition, there was a model for the public provision of health care working very well in a country that was quite similar to the United States. While there is no reliable public opinion data available for this time, it is not difficult to imagine that the turbulence underlying the health policy arena was suitable for the potential of a new health care policy to erupt—a new policy that would transform health care from a private good to a public right. All that would be required is some level of advocacy that would bring the turbulence to an evolutionary state.

The presidents of the modern era of politics (1933 to the present) frequently met this challenge. Beginning with President Franklin Roosevelt's halted attempt to append national health care to the Social Security Act and continuing through President Harry Truman's term, the president acted as an advocate for changing how Americans pay for health care. Many of these proposals were abandoned along the way. However, in 1965, President Lyndon Johnson successfully advocated for the passage of Medicare and Medicaid legislation. When those acts were signed into law, the nature of health care did indeed change and the federal and state governments became providers of comprehensive health insurance for large segments of the population.

Until this point, the United States had relied on a free-market system for the provision of health care. As I have noted, some Americans entered into collective markets for health care generally through employer-sponsored health insurance. However, other than the military health care systems and the Indian Health Service, there had never been a large-scale publicly funded health care system. Thus, the adoption of Medicare and Medicaid represents a clear departure from the course that had been pursued in the 180 years of the republic. The reasons, nested in public opinion and the overall political context that gave rise to these programs, are addressed more fully in chapter 3. However, without giving away the story, it is important to discuss the institutional component of Medicare and Medicaid, for as Baumgartner and Jones (1993) and North (1990) state, institutions are the stabilizing forces in public policy. Thus, in order for policies to change, there must be institutional flexibility, or a desire to abandon existing institutions. Likewise, for a policy to endure, there must be some sort of institutional structure associated with the policy. Clearly, the United States had never experimented with national health care for the general public—not even for a segment of the population based on age or income, thus there was no existing institution.

Nevertheless, there was an institution that had oftentimes been the subject of advocacy efforts to provide national health insurance (see chapter 3), the Social Security Administration. Thus, it should come as no surprise, given the path dependent nature of health care policy in the United States, that the first major federal foray into the provision of health insurance would bring about the creation of an institution within the Social Security Administration. So it was that in time the Health Care Financing Administration (HCFA) was established to administer and regulate the Medicare program as well as to assist states in the administration of Medicaid. Since then, HCFA's goals have been to control costs while ensuring high quality and universal access. These goals are, in some regard, mutually exclusive. For example, universal access makes cost control much more difficult. However, these objectives remain extremely popular with both elites and the public. In this book, HCFA's goals, along with their resonance among policy elites and the public, are examined in order to answer the question of why the modern era is dominated by a constant motivation to change health care policy in the United States.

Beginning with one of the two major goals of HCFA—health care cost control—it is not surprising that the cost of health care often drives the political debate. For example, rising health care costs in the early 1970s were followed by the passage of the Health Maintenance Organization (HMO) Act in 1973. The most recent episode of efforts to reform the health care system arose, at least in part, because of the cost to individuals of health care and the inability of many to obtain health insurance. For example, Jacobs and Shapiro (2000) note that "Clinton embraced health care reform in order to control costs" (110). Throughout 1993 and 1994, President Clinton continuously emphasized cost control as an impetus for health care reform. Although Clinton quickly diminished the emphasis, in accordance with his adviser's wishes, cost remained "the paramount issue in Clinton's mind" (111). Overall, health care costs in the United States were then, and still are, rising at an increasing rate. In 1965, for example, health care expenditures consumed approximately 6% of the gross domestic product while they currently consume approximately three times as much. This affects both state and federal governments, given that 17% of children and 5% of adults (about 30.5 million people in total) are enrolled in Medicaid. For example, between 1970 and 1993 the state share of Medicaid spending rose from $2.5 billion (constant) to $41.8 billion (constant) (Levit, Lazenty & Sivarajan, 1994). Weissert and Weissert (1996) have noted that, "in 1992 state Medicaid expenses took up 34 percent of the state budget in New Hampshire, 28 percent in Rhode Island, 24 percent in Tennessee, 23 percent in New York and Louisiana, and 21 percent in Indiana and Missouri. . . . [B]y fiscal year 1993 the mean state spending for Medicaid exceeded state spending for higher education . . . by $2 billion" (p. 208). The problem also exists at the federal level with 30% of the federal budget dedicated to Medicare and Medicaid, and plans to ensure the solvency of these programs dominate the debate over the uses of the newfound federal surplus.

The basic problem of ever-increasing health care costs rests in the simple equation that generates costs:

$$(\text{Price}) \times (\text{Quantity}) = \text{Costs}$$

As with all equations containing variables, one can change or fix the value of these components. Such manipulations will, in theory, alter the output of the function.

Attempts to limit the variables in this equation, price and quantity, could be achieved through various regulatory mechanisms. For example, government could impose price controls, and freeze the price at some level. The problem with this solution is that the enterprising hospital or physician could simply increase the quantity of services performed, thereby keeping the output (costs) level. In the same sense, raising prices could circumvent attempts to limit quantity (rationing). Thus, any regulatory attempt to control costs must place limits on both the price of medical services and the quantity. This then affects the other two ideals established under HCFA, quality and access. To control cost, price or quantity must be changed. If quantity is changed through rationing, then access decreases. If price decreases through cost controls, then quality suffers, either because quantity increases or because highly skilled health care providers pursue other, more lucrative careers.

Nevertheless, the recognition that costs can be controlled only through rationing and global budgeting is crucial to the success of state-sponsored health care plans. For example, the British National Health Service has a budget frozen at 6% of the gross domestic product of the United Kingdom (Aaron & Schwartz, 1984). The means of achieving this control is through price control in the form of global budgeting and restrictions on the quantity supplied through rationing.

In the United States, the federal government, through HCFA, has adopted two programs designed to control health care costs. The first is the Diagnostic Related Group (DRG), a fee schedule designed to control hospital expenditures; the other is the Resource Based Relative Value Scale (RBRVS), which is an attempt to control physician costs within the fee-for-service system used in both Medicare and Medicaid. Despite these efforts, health care costs continue to rise.

Two pioneering states, Arizona and Oregon, attempted variations on the British approach to control their own spending through Section 1115 Demonstration Waivers. In these states there was recognition that operating government-funded health insurance plans on a fee-for-service basis created many of the cost control problems that are present in private fee-for-service arrangements. Primarily, cost shifting by the hospitals and physician-induced demand (Chard 2003).

Cost shifting occurs when individuals without private health insurance who are ineligible for traditional Medicaid benefits seek care. The bills go unpaid and are absorbed by the hospital or the physician who then pass the costs along to insured individuals through increased rates. The second is a long held assumption among health economists (see Feldstein, 1993, for example) that physicians who are paid on a quantity-based scale push quantity up by ordering more tests and procedures. In managed care arrangements, physician-induced demand is controlled, while universal coverage solves the problem of cost shifting.

RBRVS, DRG, and the Demonstration Waivers all show efforts to reform health care without departing too far from existing policies. The RBRVS and DRG programs were introduced within HCFA programs initially but quickly made their way into the private sector. Likewise, the Demonstration Waivers were initially experiments by Arizona and Oregon that were quickly adopted universally by other states (Chard, 2003). Within the HCFA, health care policy reform designed to control costs was introduced into both the public and the private component of health care. To a great extent, this is what one would expect in a health care system that developed like the one in the United States. Although government intervention did occur, the intervention was used merely to cure a failure in the existing market (i.e., the poor and the elderly could not participate in collective health insurance purchasing groups). Additionally, the intervention created an institution that not only provided stability to the policy scene, but also provided a mechanism to reform health care in the private market.

THE DYNAMIC NATURE OF HEALTH CARE REFORM?

The political environment necessarily intertwines the political nature of health care with health policy in the United States. It seems that in the modern political era, health care policy and the role of government in health care are never quite settled in the United States. Other countries have chosen public provision of health care as a general policy. However, in the United States, there is a constant tension between those who believe that health care is a public good and those who believe that health care is a private good. As a result, the establishment of health care policy has emerged as a dynamic process. In this book, the role of the public in the health care saga is examined by presenting a series of snapshots of health care policy from various perspectives, ranging from the role of presidents as advocates for increased federal financing of health care to the controls placed on federal spending by citizen ideology. Within this examination, there is a common thread tying together public opinion in all of its various incarnations and addressing how public opinion influences public policy, and how public opinion is, in turn, influenced by public policy, politicians, the media, and myriad other factors. The overall goal is to gain understanding of the underlying turbulence beneath the surface of what we view as a stable policy area that gives rise to the volcanic eruptions that usher in an evolutionary change in policy.

Health care is used as a policy area because it is consistently viewed as one of the most important issues and the debate over the role of the federal government is not yet settled. The turbulence that exists in health care policy is truly a product of the modern era of politics. It is nested in the debates over big national government versus a reliance on state and local government; whether laissez-faire free-market approaches are the best solution for a multitude of problems; and, most important for this book, the questions What role can public opinion play? What role does public opinion play and is that role predictable? To answer these questions, the nature of health care policy must be investigated more thoroughly.

To this point, I have discussed health care policy in the United States as conforming, in general, to a path dependent model (North, 1990). To demonstrate this, I have discussed elements of health care policy in a historical perspective and showed how the course of health care policy in the United States relates to a path dependent system. Beyond that, I have suggested that health care policy is also susceptible to events of discontinuous change that represent an evolutionary advancement in terms of health care policy. This relies on an explanation of health care as a dynamic policy area that has a degree of turbulence beneath the surface, constantly bringing the path of health care to a state where reform can, and in some cases does, occur. I argue that one way to capture this dynamic, and understand the true nature of the turbulence, is to examine public opinion and its constituent components. However, it is critical for this discussion that the identity of health care policy as a dynamic area is understood.

Activity, in terms of health care reform efforts, is based on three crucial elements of politics in America. First, is the overall importance of health care. Consistently, polls rate health care in the top ten concerns of the American public. Thus, it is a political issue. Intertwined with this is the second element, the debate over whether health care is a public good or a private good. Finally, federal and state interventions in health care through Medicare and Medicaid are attempts to not only change the mix of public and private provision of health care, but also, as discussed earlier, to establish enduring institutions through which health care policy can be altered. This goes far to explain the dynamic nature of health care policy. Which of these aspects of health care is emphasized is *context dependent*—that is, it is determined by the ideology of the times and the citizens and elites involved. Because of the emphasis on context, much of the activity in health care policy is an attempt to change the rules of the game, to redefine policy space so that health care will become more public or private depending on the goals of the agents for change. It is in this way that politicians, political entrepreneurs, and institutions enter the arena to change health care policy.

To understand this dynamic process of policy change, health care policy is investigated through different lenses that focus on various aspects of the process of creating health care policy, all based in attitudes held by the actors. There is a general attention to efforts to move policy space by the president, the role of public opinion in the creation of health policy, and a unique attempt to preserve the private nature of health care within a government-operated market.

This relationship is depicted in Figure 2.1, which shows the dynamics of health care policy in terms of the participants in the process. If one thinks of health care policy as being in a punctuated equilibrium system such that the public provision and private provision of health care are held in some sort of stasis that is only stable for short periods of time, one can understand the dynamic nature of health care. The underlying current is the public, both individually and in collective organizations. These citizens and groups have preferences for the provision of health care that are anchored at the two ideological extremes, pure public provision and (nearly) pure private provision. This debate influences politicians from the president to Congress at the national level and governors and legislators at the state level to propose, promote, and implement policy changes that shift the equilibrium toward more public provision or more private provision of health care.

To understand how health care policy has evolved in the United States, it is first necessary to understand the general nature of policy change. Scholars studying policy change are of two schools of thought: Those who believe that change can be dynamic (e.g., Baumgartner & Jones, 1993; Schneider & Teske with Mintrom 1995) and those who believe that policy change is incremental (e.g., North 1990). While the adherents of the former school see policy change as quick and decisive, the latter see policy change as an evolutionary process. The argument that changes in health care policy exhibit both characteristics is presented throughout this book. In one sense, it is incremental, advancing slowly, as was the case during the New Deal and the Fair Deal as well as in more recent times during the Clinton administration. On the other hand, it is dynamic, with rapid change occurring in 1965 with the passage of Medicare and Medicaid and more recently with the shift to Medicaid managed care.

The overall debate between these views of policy change is based in a discussion of institutions. The preceding paragraphs refer to institutions as entities that stabilize policy, however, at this point in the discussion, that definition becomes too simplistic. Thus, before continuing, a working definition is in order. North's (1990) definition of institutions is broad and aqueous and is thus one that is useful for framing the discussion that follows without constraining it:

> [A]ny form of constraint that human beings devise to shape human interaction. Are institutions formal or informal? They can be either . . .

Figure 2.1
A Conceptual Model of the Potential for Policy Change

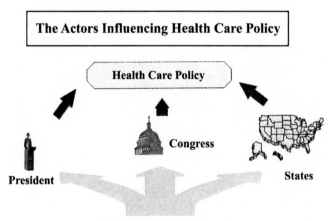

formal constraints—such as rules that human beings devise—and . . . informal constraints—such as conventions and codes of behavior. Institutions may be created, as was the United States Constitution; or they may simply evolve over time, as does the common law. (p. 4)

Thus, in North's definition, institutions can change either through creation or evolution. Much of his research is dedicated to the notion of path dependence that is an evolutionary perspective on changing institutions. North argues that policy change as defined by institutional change is incremental. On the surface, in North's view, institutions are stable. However, "from conventions, codes of conduct, and norms of behavior to statute law, and common law, and contracts between individuals, institutions are evolving and therefore, are continually altering the choices available to us" (p. 6). As North notes, this fits within the policy entrepreneur framework: "[I]ncremental change comes from the perceptions of the entrepreneurs in political and economic organizations that they could do better by altering the existing institutional framework at some margin" (p. 8). I will explain this further in chapter 3.

Other incremental theorists explain these alterations at the margins as imitations of past success. For example, Alchian (1950) explains that imitation of past success while marginally adapting the strategy to suit the current situation is a rational response to an uncertain environment. Alchian writes in support of the path dependent system:

[E]ven innovation is accounted for by imitation. While there are certainly those who consciously innovate, there are those who, in their imperfect attempts to imitate others, unconsciously innovate by unwittingly acquiring some unexpected or unsought unique attributes which under prevailing circumstances prove partly responsible for success. (pp. 218–219)

Alchian provides the foundation, in this sense, for North's notion of policy change. Alchian's system is one in which policy change occurs because of innovation and adaptation to a slowly changing environment, rather than through radical shifts. He bases the idea in the notion that it is a rational response to uncertainty: "[U]ncertainty provides an excellent reason for imitation of observed success. . . . [I]t accounts for uniformity among survivors, derived from an evolutionary, adopting, competitive system employing a criterion of survival, which can operate independently of individual motivations" (p. 219).

Other economic theorists examining policy change explore this notion. For example, Nelson and Winter (1982) discuss the notion of constraints placed on institutional change by organizational memory or, the "operational knowledge" of the institution. This, the authors argue, constrains institutions and prevents dynamic change in favor of evolutionary change.

McFarland (1991) augments the notion of simple evolutionary advancement by examining the possibility that the cyclical activity of interest groups drives change. He sees cycles of activity by these interest groups working within a system that is advancing ever so slowly toward a definite goal. This view is supportive of McClosky and Zaller's (1984) assertion that while U.S. politics undergoes cycles of increased democracy and increased capitalism, overall, the advancement has been steadily moving toward democracy. In contrast, Carmines and Stimson (1986) argue that this is simply a matter of the dynamic process that causes issues to be placed on the agenda. Rather than an overall evolution of thought, these authors see policy change as a natural result of "the joint transformation of issues and party systems" (p. 901).

This latter view is reminiscent of the notion of a dynamic policy entrepreneur guiding the evolution of policy. The notion that policy change is and can be dynamic is championed by Baumgartner and Jones (1993) who argue:

Even a casual observer of the public agenda can easily note that public attention to social problems is anything but incremental. Rather, issues have a way of grabbing headlines and dominating the schedules of public officials when they were virtually ignored only weeks or months before. Policy action may or may not follow attention, but when it does, it will not flow incrementally. In scholarly literature on agenda-setting, incrementalism plays little role. Rather, focusing events, chance occurrences, public-opinion campaigns by organized interests, and speeches by public officials are seen to cause issues to shoot high on the agenda in a short period. (p. 10).

The authors go on to argue that "any study of the dynamics of American political institutions must be able to account for long periods of stability and short, violent periods of change . . . with respect to the processing of issues, not in the basic constitutional framework" (p. 4). Baumgartner and Jones develop a theory of agenda setting that takes into account the incrementalism that North observes while arguing that a dynamic system can exhibit incremental characteristics: "[D]eliberate incrementalism allows a system to maintain a dynamic equilibrium with its environment" (p. 10). At the center of the deliberate incrementalism is the policy entrepreneur, an individual who moves policy. In Kingdon's (1984) view, policy entrepreneurs have a stockpile of solutions that they attach to rising problems that are politically important. Polsby (1984) adds to this by using a case study approach to illuminate the role of an individual entrepreneur in manipulation of a policy situation.

Riker (1986) advances the basic notion by applying a systematic element to the concept of policy entrepreneurs. He identifies three areas in which entrepreneurs act: agenda control, strategic voting, and dimensionality. The first two coincide with the common notion of agenda control through manipulation of the rules, while the third addresses control through altering the terms of the debate.

Together, these authors build the foundation of the view that policy change is and can be dynamic. Schneider and Teske (1992, 1993, 1995) discuss the characteristics of policy entrepreneurs and their role in dynamic policy change. While they concentrate on local governments, their basic underlying assumptions about entrepreneurs are applicable to national policy issues.

The authors (1995) rely on the work of economists from the Austrian school, building their analyses of policy entrepreneurs on Schumpeter's basic notion: "[T]hat the 'creative destruction' resulting from entrepreneurial activity is a mainspring of capitalism. Thus, despite the success or failure of individual entrepreneurs, their actions generate considerable benefits for society as a whole" (p. 7). This is a slightly different interpretation of Alchian's (1950) idea that innovation is less an example of risk taking than it is a rational reaction to uncertainty. The authors conclude that entrepreneurs play a complex role in dynamic policy change, creating opportunities by "changing policy ideas, changing consumer/citizen preferences, changing technology. . . . [E]ntrepreneurs seize the opportunities that emerge when citizen demand for change increases, but entrepreneurs also create *new* opportunities and mobilize citizen demand to support a fresh vision of the future" (p. 222).

This notion of dynamic change is supported by Roberts and King (1996) who argue that the literature assuming that policy change proceeds in an evolutionary fashion is misguided. They instead argue that "events, by themselves, do not automatically produce change: crises can be ignored, shocks can be weathered, jolts can be minimized. The potential for radical change by design occurs when someone defines the situation, interprets the crisis, constructs an explanation of what it means, and describes how to deal with it" (p. 222). To them, the person responsible for change is a policy entrepreneur, which they define as one who "design[s] interventions and formulate[s] political strategies to overcome the resistance of [his] opponents" (p. 242).

In sum, one can view the schools of thought concerning policy change as dynamism versus incrementalism. The dynamic notion assumes that individuals, acting as policy entrepreneurs, seek to change existing policy. As the name implies, it is an active process, driven by policy entrepreneurs. In contrast, the evolutionary approach views policy change as an incremental system. While it is flexible enough to incorporate the ideas of policy entrepreneurs, the system relies on gradual change over time; although, it can also support the notion that policy is like a perpetual motion machine, continuing along a certain path until some exterior vent forces a correction in the course.

INCREMENTALISM VERSUS DYNAMISM IN HEALTH CARE

Nevertheless, as the path dependent model predicts, only fundamental changes in the interests of society results in nonincremental deviations from the path. Thus, the seemingly random shocks in the path dependent system or the punctuated equilibria in the dynamic system can be viewed as the mediating effect of the public or the instigating effect of politicians. Jacobs and Shapiro (2000) hint at this: "Congressional efforts to lead public opinion solve the puzzle of legislators simultaneously discounting public opinion on health care reform while acknowledging that their reelection would be affected by their constituents' preferences toward it. Legislators defused the threat to reelection by working to move the public toward supporting their positions and simulating responsiveness" (p. 128).

Thus, the mediating effect of public opinion on health care policy can be summed up as the ability of public preferences to change policy at the margins. Likewise, the instigating effect of politicians and elites is simply their efforts at all levels to persuade members of the public that the policies that these elites endorse are indeed in the best interest of the public. To that extent, public opinion is influenced by elite rhetoric (Zaller, 1992).

In terms of politics, health care policy is a perennial topic. It has consistently ranked among the chief policy concerns of the American public in Gallup opinion polls since the 1960s, as well it should. Health care consumes more than one seventh of the overall gross national product of the United States, a greater percentage than any other industrialized country. This is in part because, as Aaron (1991) notes, Americans are enamored of high tech and acute care; thus, these preferences are a product of the culture of the United States (Starr, 1982). While, these cultural preferences result in phenomenal costs and rapidly growing rates for health care expenditures in the United States, they are also a component of the context within which the debate over health care reform takes place. Therefore, the public component of health care policy is itself a saga that is wrapped in the turbulence that lies beneath existing health care policy in the United States.

Broadly, the studies presented in the following chapters demonstrate how the attitudes of the public and the elites influence health care policy and public spending. Substantively, these concepts are used to examine specific questions. Specifically, how did the Clinton Health Security Act fail despite a very promising debut in September 1993 when, as Jacobs and Shapiro (2000) have noted, "independent polls reported that nearly 60 percent favored Clinton's plan. . . . Gallup surveys showed that . . . Democrats supported it overwhelmingly (83 percent to 13 percent) and a majority of independents also backed it (55 percent to 34 percent)" (pp. 133–134)?

Chapter 3

Path Dependence and Policy Change

Examining Public Mood and Federal Spending

INTRODUCTION

The focus of this chapter is on whether public opinion, specifically the public mood, translates into changes in federal health care spending. Budgets represent an ideal model for a path dependent system. Generally speaking, last year's budget was the best predictor of this year's budget which is, of course, the best predictor of next year's budget, and so it goes into eternity unless something occurs to change it. This is the nature of a path dependent system in that the present is a reflection of the past and a glimpse into the future, unless there is an evolutionary change in policy. In addition to presenting a functioning model of path dependence, historically, budgets have been seen as a means of promoting public policy (Lynch, 1995). This is true in health care as well. However, health care policy is, at times, a unique policy area. While it is true that there are definite ideologically grounded notions about who should finance health care (Graig ,1999; Schlesinger & Lau, 2000), there is an emotional component to the issue that is present in only a few other policy areas (education, crime, and to some extent the environment). This is true because, for many, health care is a life-and-death issue. As such, health care policy issues are consistently among the most salient (Gallup, 1994; 2001).

For many, health care is, in fact, a life-and-death issue. A diabetes diagnosis or the loss of health insurance alters the notion of security that citizens possess. For that reason, to many individuals, the important part of President Clinton's Health Security Act was the security that it would provide. In fact, Jacobs and Shapiro (2000) note that this was indeed a "selling feature" as perceived by Clinton's advisers: "Greenberg's suggestion was that the president focus on the broad goal of health care security. . . . [He] assured the White House that the 'Security for All' theme would tap Americans' support for universal coverage and be perceived as credible" (p. 107). Stimson (1999) underscores this notion of security as a resonating message, writing, "insecurity is growing rapidly in the health domain as a mounting proportion of ordinary Americans must come to grips with the knowledge that their only possibility of care when in need is to plead for free treatment. Inasmuch as this represents declining security . . . one might expect a particularly pronounced political response" (p. 82). Stimson was writing about the opinions on health care primarily in the late 1980s, when many more Americans lost their health insurance. By 1992, with 37 million uninsured, the insecurity reached epidemic proportions, and contributed in part to the election of Harris Wofford to the Senate from Pennsylvania and Bill Clinton, whose campaign promised a national health care plan, to the presidency.

It is possible to examine changes in health care policy by examining realignments of attitudes held by the public in regard to the role of government in the provision of health care. In chapter 1, I put forward the argument that health care policy in the United States was a path dependent institution, driven by ideologies of the public. This concept is based on the work of Laurene Graig (1999) who creates three categories: the national health service model, the social insurance model, and the private insurance model. Three characteristics—coverage, financing, and ownership—define the main categories of health coverage. Graig, relying on Anderson's (1989) work further arranges these systems within a market-minimized (socialist systems) versus market-maximized (capitalist systems) continuum. (See Table 3.1 for a typology of these systems.) Graig concludes that the "notion of a continuum underscores the importance of the overall political process and the decision-making roles played by the public and private sectors regarding the development of health care systems. As Anderson noted, 'the philosophy of government's counter-balancing private-sector interest groups affects the structure, financing and equity of the health services' (p. 4). Hence, we can conclude that in addition to existing institutional and political arrangements, citizen ideologies about health care policy are important in understanding how and why health policy change occurs.

To capture this dimension, it is logical to use Stimson's (1999) attitudes toward government health care spending as a proxy for adherence to one of the ideologies. Thus, an analysis of the public's influence on health care spending by government can be broadly conceived in terms of the ideologies associated with health care provision. Of course, tempering this overall attitudinal shift is the group-based theory of public policy pioneered by Lasswell (1936) and developed more fully in recent years by Ingram and Schneider (1995) and

TABLE 3.1
A Typology of Health Care Paradigms

	Coverage	Finance	Ownership	Market
National Health Service	Automatic Universal	Tax based	Public	Minimized
Social Insurance	Compulsory Universal	Employer and Individual	Public and Private	
Private Insurance	Individual Choice	Individual and/or Employer	Private	Maximized

Schneider and Ingram (1990; 1993). In this research, the authors set forth a theory that is based in pluralism, social constructions. However, in an attempt to further our understanding of the components of turbulence in path dependent systems (that create those rare opportunities for evolutionary changes in policy), I ask whether public mood and social constructions converge to create conditions that are optimal for policy change? Additionally, an equally intriguing question is What is the nature of the change, or more specifically, what is the nature of the underlying turbulence that leads to policy change?

Social constructions of target populations, which Schneider and Ingram (1993) define as "the cultural characterizations or popular images of the persons or groups whose behavior and well-being are affected by public policy. These characterizations are normative and evaluative, portraying groups in positive or negative terms through symbolic language, metaphors, and stories" (p. 334). The concept of social constructions, has been a dominant theory in the field of sociology for a number of years. In the early 1960s, Edelman (1964) described social constructions as a normative mechanism that conveys information about a group by various means, including symbolic language and metaphors. In mainstream political science, even those who trace their roots to the sociology-inspired branch of political science have largely ignored these constructions.

However, the recent work of Schlesinger and Lau (2000) brings back the notion of using metaphors to categorize beliefs or attitudes. The classification of health care based on metaphors is less concerned with how health care policy and the means to gain health care can be arranged in a typology of public and private goods, and more concerned with individual attitudes and ideologies. Thus, the metaphor-based theory presented by Schlesinger and Lau builds on the synthesized model created by Craig (1999) by adding an individual component to the typology. To that end, Schlesinger and Lau present five metaphors that can be used to describe the attitudes of the beholder and can be easily arranged along a traditional liberal to conservative continuum:

> *Health Care as a Societal Right,* available to all citizens of the country under roughly equal terms, with these terms determined collectively for the nation as a whole through the political process at the federal level;
>
> *Health Care as a Community Obligation,* also reflecting a collective obligation, though in this case defined at the local level, with each community taking responsibility only for illnesses that befall those in their geographic area, with the standards of appropriate treatment defined independently by each locality;
>
> *Health Care as an Employer Responsibility,* a variant on the community metaphor, in which the community is defined in terms of relationships in the workplace, requiring each employer to assume responsibility for all workers and their dependents, and allowing the terms of appropriate care to be defined through negotiations between workers and management in each firm;
>
> *Health Care as a Marketable Commodity,* distributed according to each person's ability to pay for medical services, with standards of care determined through individual choice and market forces; and,
>
> *Health Care as a Professional Service,* with the terms of appropriate treatment determined through scientific definitions of need, shaped through professional training, and distributed according to a combination of the client's ability to pay and some professional obligations to offer services on a pro bono basis. (p. 624)

These metaphors provide the underlying context to explore the actions and motivations of the actors—the president, the Congress, the states, interest groups, and the public—who influence health care policy development and implementation. Schlesinger and Lau's metaphors represent the individual attitudes held by the public and the elites that are aggregated at some point to form general health policy preferences. Whether one views health care as a commodity that should be publicly financed is driven by the adherence to the political beliefs described in the five health care metaphors put forth by Schlesinger and Lau. These metaphors are especially pertinent to the United States, as they encompass all possible views held by various sectors of the American public and the policy elites, and remain based in underlying attitudes toward populations.

SOCIAL CONSTRUCTIONS AND MEDICARE

Schneider and Ingram (1993) assert that "the social construction of target populations has a powerful influence on public officials and shapes both the policy agenda and the actual design of the policy" (p. 334). They further argue that the social construction of a target population not only defines a group, but can also shape that group (p. 334). Thus, one dynamic change in policy toward a certain group can have lasting effects in changing attitudes of the public toward that group. That means that once a certain group becomes the beneficiary of a public policy, the policy itself can have ripple effects throughout society that serve to solidify attitudes, either positive or negative, toward that group.

Nowhere is the positive impact of this supposition more evident than in the case of Medicare and its primary target, the elderly.[1] Since its inception, Medicare has been an example of the Schneider and Ingram supposition that while "some social constructions remain constant over a long period of time . . . others are subject to continual debate and manipulation" (p. 336). In accordance with this theory, Social Security was the first step in changing public attitudes toward the elderly (Schottland, 1963). Following that and building on it, Medicare became an empowerment tool for the elderly by dramatically and permanently changing their social construction. In contrast, Koff and Park (1999) argue that Social Security simply caused the elderly to trade their traditional dependence on the family for a dependence on government, thus leaving them firmly in a disadvantaged status. In either case, public attitudes toward the elderly changed significantly from 1935, when health insurance for the elderly was removed from the original Social Security plan, to 1965, when Medicare, a health care model that rests firmly in the most liberal of Schlesinger and Lau's (2000) metaphors was passed. (For an in-depth discussion of a negative impact of social constructions on public policy positions, see Gilens, 1999.)

HOW THE ELDERLY LOST AND REGAINED THEIR HEALTH INSURANCE

In their work on the subject, Schneider and Ingram (1993) argue that policy is designed for groups and tempered by public attitudes toward that group. In other words, policies are constructed based on attitudes of the public toward the policy, as well as attitudes toward those affected by the policy. As the authors note, because of the nature of democracy in the United States, policy designed to benefit certain groups is more easily adopted when the groups are viewed as deserving. Further, like public policy itself, these constructions can and do change, both in dynamic fashion and incrementally.

Returning to the concept of health care metaphors, one can imagine that, while the prevalent attitude in the country on the whole may be one that subscribes to the professional service metaphor, it is possible that the public will hold a different attitude when discussing health care for particular groups such as children or the elderly. For example, in the early 1960s, insurance companies were canceling policies for the elderly at alarming rates. Those elderly who remained insured were charged exorbitant premiums and quickly discontinued their insurance for financial reasons (Feldstein, 1993; Koff & Park, 1999). Political pressure from elderly advocacy groups like the National Council on Aging and the American Association of Retired Persons led to the creation of Medicare, a national health insurance program for the elderly (Koff & Park, 1999). As Koff and Park note, the advocacy efforts changed public attitudes toward the elderly as a group, transforming them from a dependent population to an advantaged population to use Schneider and Ingram's (1993) terminology.[2] Essentially, it is possible to come to the conclusion that the elderly were changed from a group viewed as deserving some assistance in terms of health care, the recipients of pro bono care in the professional service metaphor, to a group deserving a special waiver so that their health care became a societal responsibility (see Huddy, Jones, & Chard, 2001, for a similar analysis).

The elderly of America lost their health insurance in the years following World War II. This was due to a number of social factors, not the least of which was the increasing urbanization of the United States. The most significant factor, according to the general consensus, was the growth of commercial health insurance companies during World War II (Aaron, 1991). The rise of commercial health insurers has its origins in a path dependent model that began when President Roosevelt imposed wage controls during World War II. With their hands tied in regard to wages, employers began offering fringe benefits as a means of attracting employees. Health insurance was one such benefit and was often included in the package. At the time, there were few commercial insurers, because the general consensus was that health insurance was not a profitable business. The largest insurer was Blue Cross/Blue Shield, which in those days was quite different from the Blue Cross/Blue Shield we know today. Blue Cross/Blue Shield had a mission statement to insure all people, along with values based in its quasi-religious origins at Baylor University. Because of this, Blue Cross/Blue Shield assessed premiums based on a community rating system, wherein all of the insured paid the same premium, whether old or young, sick or healthy.

With the proliferation of health insurance, the commercial insurers were attracted to the market—a market dominated by Blue Cross/Blue Shield. To compete, commercial insurers began culling away younger and healthier people, enticing them to leave the community pool in exchange for lower premiums (Aaron, 1991; Feldstein, 1993). As Aaron notes, this eventually led to a community pool comprised almost entirely of ill and elderly. These pools, as Aaron and Feldstein explain, caused premiums to skyrocket and the elderly and chronically ill were eventually priced out of the market.

This situation existed when Medicare, as a stand-alone program, was first proposed in the late 1940s (Koff & Park, 1999). At that time, there were no advocates for the elderly or their interests, nor was there a cohesive lobbying group petitioning Congress on behalf of the elderly (Koff & Park, 1999). This, taken with the other socioeconomic facts known about the elderly at that time (Schottland, 1963), would place the elderly, as a group, solidly in the dependent social construction according to Schneider and Ingram's (1993) typology.

However, in 1958, the American Association of Retired Persons (AARP) was founded "to enhance the quality of life of older persons, to promote their independence, dignity and purpose, to provide leadership in determining the role and place of older persons in society, and to improve the image of aging" (Koff & Park, 1995, p. 310). Three years later, in 1961, the National Council of Senior Citizens (NCSC) was established "to advocate on behalf of the elderly and to secure a better life for older persons, consistent with national interests and to seek the passage of Medicare or some similar health insurance program for the elderly" (Koff & Park, 1995, p. 311). From this language used to describe the purpose of the AARP and the NCSC, it is possible to assemble a social construction for the elderly. By simply taking the converse of that which each group is advocating, we get a social construction of a group that is without dignity, independence, purpose, leadership, or a good way of life.

What happened next was a transformation of public opinion. As Schneider and Ingram (1993) note, "[S]ocial constructions are manipulated and used by public officials, the media, and the groups themselves. New target groups are created, and images are developed for them; old groups are reconfigured or new images created" (p. 342). With a forceful and popular advocate in the White House (see chapter 4), public opinion moved in favor of health care provision for the elderly under the societal right metaphor. As a result, a dynamic change in health care policy occurred because of a momentous change in public opinion. This change represented a clear evolutionary departure (North, 1990) from the existing health policy metaphor in the United States. Thus, the question of importance is whether, through an examination of public mood and its relationship to the path dependent system of public finance for health care, we can gain greater understanding into the elements and process that leads to these evolutionary changes in policy.

ANALYZING CHANGE

One approach to examining this relationship is through a time series analysis. The study of health care politics and policy is amenable to time series analysis because of the dynamic nature of the system and the ever-changing attitudes held by the public toward the role of government in the provision of health care. Likewise, thinking about policy in a path dependent system necessarily requires that time is taken into account. As I argued at the beginning of this chapter, budgeting presents a perfect model of path dependence because it advances incrementally over time with few exceptions. Of course, the exceptions are what make the system interesting because they represent the dynamic changes that forever alter the path dependent model of policy (North, 1990).

The path dependent nature of public health care spending is obvious when viewing a graph, like that presented in Figure 3.1, in which public health care spending is plotted against time. In looking at this figure, a picture is indeed worth a thousand words in that it reveals that public health care spending observed over a period of time is a dynamic and trending process, even when controlling for inflation. Thus, Figure 3.1 illustrates a system that follows a path dependent model, increasing, but not departing dramatically from, its origins. The incremental increases are, at times, so minute that in some cases they are almost imperceptible, and it is only in seeing the end point that one realizes there has been a dramatic change from the origin.

This gradual incremental increase has a unique effect on the entire series of observations in that it smoothes out the pattern. Although the trend is clearly upward, it is possible to conclude that there have never been any

FIGURE 3.1
Federal Health Care Spending Per Capital: 1960–1994
(in thousands of dollars)

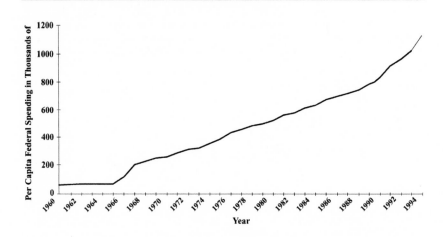

dramatic changes in public health care spending that might correlate with the sort of evolutionary change in health care policy that Medicare and Medicaid may have represented. However, if we examine changes in public spending on a year-to-year basis, it is possible to capture the dramatic changes that are lost in the bigger picture presented in Figure 3.1.

Indeed, when one examines the annual percentage change in spending, a more attention-grabbing and somewhat more dynamic series emerges as can be seen in Figure 3.2. What makes this figure interesting is the dramatic spike from 1965 to 1968 where the political intervention in the health care market, through the expenditure of federal funds, influenced the series.

The spike represents the evolutionary change in health care policy that comes along only when conditions are right for such a change. In this case, Medicare and Medicaid are responsible for the increase in federal spending on health care. Medicare and Medicaid represent a significant departure in the history of the United States from a strict adherence to the private market as the best and most efficient supplier of health insurance. Consequently, health care and health insurance began to be viewed as a societal right for the elderly. The question becomes What changed?

One possible answer to that question has already been discussed: public perceptions of the elderly changed. As the previous discussion notes, the elderly were transformed into a deserving group through advocacy efforts at various

FIGURE 3.2

Percent Change in Federal Health Care Spending: 1961–1994

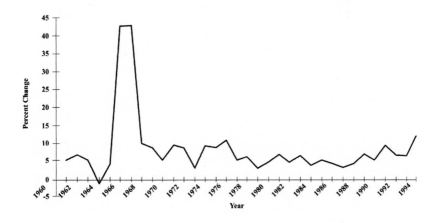

levels. However, we know from Jacobs and Shapiro's (2000) discussion of crafted talk that such a transformation does not occur in a vacuum. That is, if the public is unwilling to embrace a new spending program, regardless of the social construction of the target population, it is unlikely that the program will gain support. I have argued thus far that public opinion has the power, at least at the margins, to influence public policy and to bring about the evolutionary changes in policy within a path dependent system.

The spending measures presented in Figures 3.1 and 3.2 provide a nice glimpse of a path dependent system. However, the true interest lies in examining the turbulence beneath the system that ultimately catapults public policy in new directions. Stepping back from the simple monetary measure, it is possible to examine the turbulence, at least one component of that turbulence, by looking at the impact of public opinion. The question then moves from What changed? to Does a changing public mood translate into changing public policy? To answer this broad inquiry, I explore three specific questions. First, I investigate whether the public mood regarding health care spending (Stimson, 1999) translates into public policy, as Page and Shapiro (1992) suggest is the case. Second, I ask whether government health care spending is influenced by the attitudes of the public and if that is indeed the case, I ask What is the impact on the health care market? Finally, I investigate whether public attitudes would have supported the increase in government health care spending proposed by the Health Security Act. (See Jacobs and Shapiro, 2000, chap. 8, for a discussion of this in another context.)

To answer these questions and to explore the existence of the relationships I have posited, I use various time series estimation techniques (for a full description, please see the Methodological Appendix). First, I examine the effect of increased political involvement, through federal spending, in the private market for health care using an intervention analysis in which the adoption of Medicare in July 1966 (the implementation date) acts as the catalyst for change (the key predictor variable to examine the effect). Second, the question of whether public mood affects public spending on health care is examined using a lagged regression model (Ostrom, 1990) in which spending in the future is influenced by the mood of the population in the present.

These analyses show how public opinion on health care translates into public policy on health care. The results of the model are then used to forecast the percentage of federal spending on health care for the period from 1960 to 1994. The data used are yearly health expenditure data collected by the Congressional Budget Office and Stimson's (1999) public mood on health care.

Looking at the analysis series of observations from 1960 to 1999, it is apparent that there is a significant effect at the first period. This means that the change in health care expenditures series and the percent of total health care spending by the federal government are both processes in which the long-term effect of previous changes on the present change decays exponentially. This fits well within the path dependent nature of the system in that the best predictor of the present federal health care spending is last year's federal health care spending. In short, this analysis indicates that federal health care spending fits well within the path dependent paradigm.

Nevertheless, there are changes that cannot be explained by simply relying on an extrapolation of spending from year to year. These are dynamic changes; the reasons that they have occurred and the ability to predict conditions under which they might occur are the focus of this book. To add to our level of understanding of this process let us begin with an examination of whether Medicare did in fact represent a new equilibrium in federal health care spending.

Medicare: An Intervention Analysis

As previously mentioned, a quick glance at Figure 3.2 reveals a dramatic change in spending on health care starting in 1966 which coincides with the implementation of Medicare. Although the effect is brief, it is interesting and warrants study for two reasons: First, Medicare represents the first national health insurance plan created in the United States; and second, Medicare effectively doubled the amount of federal money spent on health care. Thus, it seems that Medicare did indeed represent an evolutionary departure from the existing health care policy path at that time.

The question thus turns to whether this intervention can be modeled, and whether the effect is significant when it is modeled. To test this, an abrupt temporary intervention model seems best (for further discussion, please see the Methodological Appendix):

$$Y_t = (\omega_0/(1 - \delta B)) * (1 - B)I_t + N_t \qquad (3.1)$$

The dependent variable (Y_t) in this system represents increases in federal health care spending, and the model itself is designed to examine whether Medicare had a significant impact on this. In many ways, this can be viewed as an original confirmatory model to support the argument that Medicare significantly changed the structure of federal spending on health care. The results show that, as expected, there was indeed a significant impact from the establishment of Medicare on federal health care spending in 1966 and 1967. Further, what is not as obvious is that bringing 20 million elderly into the health care system would affect expenditures in a "front-loaded manner." That is, as the elderly first entered the health care system, there was a high probability that acute care would be needed because of their deteriorating health after years without medical insurance (Koff & Park, 1999). Based on the strength of

TABLE 3.2

Abrupt Temporary Intervention Model for Medicare and Medicaid
on the Percentage Change in Federal Health Care Spending

	Coefficients
Constant	4.22
	(1.91)
1966	3.40
	(0.58)
Decay Rate (δ)	0.46
	(0.03)
AR(1)	0.84
	(0.12)
RMSE	60.51
Q	15

the model, the process is indeed path dependent, and it is clear that the past budget is not driving the system entirely.

Substantively, this model suggests that the effect of Medicare was a 34% increase in federal health care spending. However, the rapid and dramatic increase of 34% was a one-time event. This is shown by the decay rate, which indicates that the effect of the increases dissipated completely by 1968 and federal health care spending settled back into the incremental increases that had characterized it previously. Looking at Table 3.2, this result is clearly shown, with the percentage change in health care spending moving to a lower point through to 1972. In fact, during this period, Medicare spending increased at a slower rate than private sector health care spending (Congressional Budget Office, 1995). Thus, in 1968, following the dynamic change precipitated by Medicare in 1966 and 1967, federal health care spending settled back into a path dependent system, increasing only incrementally.

Understanding Federal Health Care Spending

The next task is to understand the dynamic process behind federal health care spending. The question that we, as political scientists, are most interested in is whether there is some connection between the public and federal health care spending. One can hypothesize many effects, both direct and indirect. For example, elections that are based on health care policy as a primary and salient issue may translate into a change in health care policy at the federal level (Conley, 2001; Jacobs & Shapiro, 2000). I am interested in examining a more fundamental aspect: attitude or what Stimson (1999) calls the "public mood." Is it true, as Page and Shapiro (1992) assert and Erikson, Wright, and McIver (1993) show that public mood translates into public policy at the state level? To test this notion, a time series analysis is important because it is necessary to capture the dynamic effect of attitude and policy change.

I use a Cochrane–Orcutt lagged regression model (Ostrom, 1990) to estimate the following model:

Federal Health Care Spending$_t$ = Health Policy Mood$_t$ +
Federal Health Care Spending$_{t-1}$ + N$_t$ (3.2)

Table 3.3 illustrates the results of this model. A one-unit change toward liberalism (generally interpreted as public opinion in favor of increased spending) results in an increase of approximately 5% in federal spending. The interesting feature of the Cochrane–Orcutt method is that the impact of the lagged variable, the variable representing previous time periods, and the independent predictor variable can be measured using the following formula:[3]

$$C_i = b_1 b_2^i$$

Thus, at two lags, the effect is :

$$C_2 = b_1 b_2^2 = (0.048) * (.837)^2 = 0.034$$

The cumulative effect over all lags is calculated as:

$$\frac{b_1}{(1 - b_2)}$$

In this case, it equals :

$$\frac{.048}{(1 - 0.837)} = 0.294$$

This means that, overall, the cumulative impact of a one-unit move toward liberalism in the public mood on health care translates into a change in federal health care spending of approximately 29% in constant dollars over a 25-year period. Thus, one would expect that had the attitudes of the public toward

TABLE 3.3
Regression Results with Federal Health Care Spending as a Percentage
of Health Care Spending as Dependent Variable (Cochrane–Orcutt
Regression Technique) $N = 34$

	β	SE
Health Policy Mood	4.977**	2.231
Percent Federal Spending (One Lag)	3.652	7.131
$SE = 1.76$		
Durbin–Watson $= 1.25$		
$R^2 = 0.99$		

$^*p < .10;\ ^{**}p < .05;\ ^{***}p < .001$

health care spending continued to become increasingly liberal following the passage of Medicare and Medicaid, the expenditures on these programs would be 29% higher than in 1966. In fact, in constant dollars, in 1991, federal health care spending was approximately 20 percentage points higher than in 1966. Thus, it is clear that at least at the margins public opinion has an impact on one measure of public policy, spending at the federal level. In this case, the public mood proves to be an important predictor of federal health care spending.

Forecasting

To examine the utility of this model, it is helpful to look at it in terms of explanatory powers and its predictive ability. For example, the model demonstrates what influences federal health care spending—the budget from the previous year, and the general feelings of the public about health care spending. This fits well within Wildavsky's (1986) description of budgets as 90–95% "locked in as a consequence of past commitments and present promises" (p. 29) and matches the path dependent theory of public policy. However, there is another important feature of budgeting, the future. As Wildavsky notes, "budgets . . . become links between financial resources and human behavior" (p. 3). The budget is a link between the public, politicians, and policy. Thus, in this model, public spending is influenced not only by past spending, but also by the will of the people. To test whether this model can predict the future based on these factors, I attempt to forecast spending from the final observations of the public mood (1989) to see how well this model predicts actual spending.

Using this simple model to forecast future federal spending on health care, I find that that overall the model was able to predict federal spending on health

FIGURE 3.3
Actual and Predicted Public Health Care Spending: 1960–1994

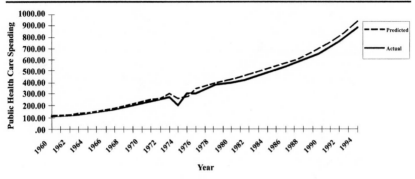

care quite well. As Figure 3.3 shows, the overall error is small. I should note that Stimson's (1999) public mood on health care measure begins in 1964 and ends in 1996, thus the first three observations use a weighted size of government score, weighted by the correlation between health care mood and size of government mood in successive years.

Implications of the Previous Model

The implications of this forecast model are apparent. Federal spending on health care, like most government spending, is constrained by previous budgets, an indication of path dependence. Thus, the budget in this case presents the sort of institutional structure that North (1990) discusses as a suppressor to dramatic change. To those who study the federal budgetary process, this observation is intuitive. However, as Burkhead (1959) noted, budgets are not only "an instrument for consciously influencing the economic life of the nation," but they are also a reflection of the "prevailing attitudes toward the role and responsibility of government" (pp. 59–60). Thus, it is not surprising that one can accurately predict federal health care spending as a percentage of total health care spending in the United States based on two observations: the previous year's spending and the public mood toward health care. Attitudes of the public toward health, which correlate with Schlesinger and Lau's (2000) metaphors, obviously translate into spending decisions at the federal level. Thus, the incremental (past budgets) and dynamic (public mood) nature of health care policy change are represented.

Ironically, despite the desire among the population for government-sponsored health insurance, as indicated by Gallup Poll results in 1992, the forecast model and actual data presented fail to find public support for increased spending (but see Jacobs and Shapiro, 2000, pp. 227–228). Thus, relying solely on attitudes of the public toward health care spending at the federal level, one could have predicted the defeat of the Health Security Act. Given that the Act would have effectively tripled federal health care spending, it is quite possible that it failed because it could not gain support among the public for the massive increase in spending.

DOES THE MOOD REALLY MATTER?

A possible challenge to the assertions made from the previous model is whether the mood really matters. One could argue that rather than the mood of the public truly determining federal health care spending, the driving force was really only the previous budget. In other words, the inclusion of the mood is simply a confounding circumstance and has no predictive or explanatory power without the control for the previous year's federal health care spending.

Testing this theory is possible, using the following model:

$$\text{Federal Health Care Spending}_t = \text{Health Policy Mood}_t + N_t \quad (3.3)$$

In this model, the effect of health policy mood on federal health care spending stands alone. Thus, I examine the impact of the public mood without taking into account the spending level from the previous year.

TABLE 3.4

Regression Results with Federal Health Care Spending as a Percentage of Health Care Spending as Dependent Variable (Cochrane–Orcutt Regression Technique) $N = 34$

	β	SE
Health Policy Mood	11.21***	2.797
Constant	−57.14***	16.463
$SE = 6.65$		
Durbin Watson $= 1.25$		
$R^2 = 0.99$		

***$p < .001$

Table 3.4 presents the results of the estimation of this model. Clearly, the impact of the mood on federal health care spending increases when I remove the lagged spending variable, rising from an average increase of approximately 5% for a one-point liberal movement in the mood to an average increase of approximately 11% absent the control for prior spending.

Of course, one could argue that this result is spurious because the most rapid increases in federal health care spending (Medicare and Medicaid) coincide with liberal times in the United States. Thus, the question is whether these results stand if the observations for 1966 and 1967 were not present. Table 3.5 presents the results of such an analysis. The impact of the mood is in fact diminished; however, it remains statistically and substantively significant. Overall, with the observations for 1966 and 1967 removed, the effect of public mood on average is a 2% increase in federal spending on health care for each one-point move in the liberal direction in public mood, while this is less than half of the estimations that include 1966 and 1967, it demonstrates an important finding that goes back to Schneider and Ingram's (1993) social construction theory, as well as the Schlesinger and Lau (2000) metaphors of health care. In this case, removing 1966 and 1967 also removes Medicare and the ameliorating effects that program had for the social construction of the elderly (Koff & Park, 1999). Likewise, the removal of 1966 and 1967 take away a period when people were more likely to embrace health care as a societal right (Schlesinger and Lau, 2000). The results also demonstrate one more important fact, this period is one of those unique opportunities when the various components of the turbulence that underlies the health policy system in the United States converged to create a dynamic and evolutionary change in health care policy.

TABLE 3.5

Regression Results with Federal Health Care Spending as a Percentage of Health Care Spending as Dependent Variable Excluding 1966 and 1967 (Cochrane–Orcutt Regression Technique) = 32

	β	SE
Health Policy Mood	1.93*	1.033
Constant	−5.18	5.988
$SE = 2.292$		
Durbin–Watson = 1.25		
$R^2 = 0.99$		

*$p < .10$.

CONCLUSION

This result shows that the public mood does in fact influence public spending on health care. Thus, public mood can, at least at the margins, influence evolutionary changes in health care policy. We know that within the policy metaphor framework, the liberal metaphors correlate to greater public provision of health care. Thus, it is logical to come to the conclusion that as the population becomes more liberal, increased public spending on health care will be favored and this will eventually translate into higher federal spending on health care, both in the presence and the absence of controls for budgets from previous years.

Nevertheless, the story of health policy change is definitely affected by more than public opinion alone. Although, it is undeniable that public opinion is indeed one of the components of the turbulence that propels policy change, it is not the only component and it certainly does not exist in a vacuum. In chapter 4, I add a level of complexity to the model: I introduce the president as a player in transforming policy. I utilize the fact that presidents have been advocates for many of the major health policy changes that have either been enacted or, at a minimum, proposed between 1952 and 1996. Within that context I model the process that leads to presidential proposals and, in some cases, policy change. This gives greater insight into the conditions that push health care policy from one station along a path dependent model to another.

Chapters 5, 6, and 7 present attitudinally based analyses of the failure of the Clinton plan. These analyses again dissect the influence of the public on policy outcomes by exploring information and persuasion models that are based in public attitudes toward government. Together, these present a comprehensive look at the factors leading to the defeat of the Health Security Act.

Chapter 4

Presidents as Advocates, Entrepreneurs, and Agenda Setters

Comparing the Success of Medicare and the Failure of the Health Security Act

INTRODUCTION

In the previous chapter, the path dependent nature of health care policy was examined by using federal health care spending as a model. Within this context, it was easy to observe evolutionary changes in health care policy because they coincided with major increases in spending. This relationship was captured at first with a simple intervention model. Then, adding a layer of complexity to the model, I estimated the impact of the public mood, as a representation of public opinion. In building the model of the path dependent system, I relied on theories of social constructions (Schneider & Ingram, 1993) and health care metaphors (Schlesinger & Lau, 2000) which themselves are nested within reciprocal relationships between public opinion and public policy. Generally speaking, the analyses in chapter 3 presented a model of the turbulence that underlies the policy system that can, at times, when conditions are right, lead to dramatic changes in policy. The turbulence is, of course, much more complex than that and it is driven by presidents, politicians, and citizens.

In 1992 health care was an increasingly salient issue, second only to the economy in Gallup's "Most Important Issue Survey" (Gallup, 2000). It was true that there was some level of dissatisfaction with health care in the United States: Gallup surveys placed it at approximately 18% compared with about

70% satisfied (Gallup, 2000). Of course, given the path dependent nature of health care policy in the United States, the question is whether that dissatisfaction was great enough to support an evolutionary change in the way the United States provides health care for its citizens. Clearly, based on the Wofford victory and their own polling, the Clinton–Gore campaign thought it was. As Jacobs and Shapiro (2000) write, "health reform rose to the top of Clinton's agenda because he and his advisers identified it as a means for achieving his overriding goals of economic rejuvenation and deficit reduction" (p. 79). The theory behind it was simple: Health care was one of the last unresolved national issues and a Democrat who was able to point to an accomplishment akin to Roosevelt's Social Security program had the potential to reclaim the White House for Democrats for years to come. However, as history demonstrates, health care is the last unresolved issue because it is complex and often takes years of advocacy to achieve incremental policy changes. Thus, the story of presidential advocacy and the pursuit of health reform by the presidents is one that is controlled to a large extent by the nature of the turbulence that underlies seemingly stable policy areas. This is a product of the times and the political environment defines those times. An important component of that environment is public opinion and the unique relationship that presidential rhetoric and public opinion enjoy. Jacobs and Shapiro (2000) note, "responsiveness to public opinion did not put [health care] on his agenda, though public attitudes reinforced Clinton's interest in health care" (p. 79). Thus, one important component is public opinion, but direct attitudes toward specific policies seem relevant only at the margins. What seems more relevant to policy change is the ability of the president to influence public opinion.

The presidential scholar Neustadt (1990) quoted President Truman as saying "that the power of the president is the power to persuade" (p. 28). In matters of policy, the president's ability to persuade the public and members of Congress along with other elites is his greatest advantage. However, as Neustadt notes, this is an advantage only if the president has the "ability to recognize the preconditions and the chance advantages and proceed accordingly in the course of choice making that comes his way" (p. 49). In this respect, presidents have the power to act as policy entrepreneurs by defining and framing policy debates (Kingdon, 1984; Riker, 1986). This chapter examines how successful the president is at the "bully pulpit" to act as an agenda setter and entrepreneur (Kernell, 1986). First, however, we need a definition for a policy entrepreneur. Generally, a policy entrepreneur can be defined as a politically motivated individual who seeks to create sweeping dynamic policy changes, as opposed to those who seek to incrementally advance policy (see, for example, Baumgartner & Jones, 1993; Kingdon, 1984; Polsby, 1984). Policy entrepreneurs do this by trying to sell their ideas to political elites, especially to members of Congress. Thus, it is not difficult to imagine a president acting as an entrepreneur in seeking to advance his policy goals (see Fett, 1992; 1994).

PRESIDENTS AS ADVOCATES AND ENTREPRENEURS

The fundamental questions this research seeks to answer are When does a president pursue policy change? When does a president succeed in changing policy? What role, if any, does public opinion play in this calculus? Conley (2001) addresses these questions to some extent:

> Elections change national policy in two ways. First, turnover can shift the policy preferences of those in office; a new cast of characters yields new policy directions. Second, electoral campaigns and outcomes can signal public enthusiasm for policy change, and elected officials can respond with changes in the national policy agenda, whether or not those changes match their personal policy preferences. . . . Presidents gauge support in Congress, and they look to the election outcome to read public support for their agenda. (p. 11)

Within this summation of presidential agenda setting, there are important considerations: Which aspects of the political world in which a president serves lead that president to propose a policy change? Which factors within that arena determine the ultimate fate of a presidential proposal? To that end, the attitudinal component of the political environment is examined. Specifically, the focus is placed on the ideology of the president (*Presidential Liberalism*[1]) and the public (*Health Policy Attitude*), along with other measures of public opinion (*Presidential Popularity; Climate*) to explain when and how presidents propose policy change (*Proposed*) and what influences the ultimate outcome of these proposals (*Policy Approved*). For the purposes of this discussion, the entrepreneur, in this case the president, can be viewed as the catalyst for change. In that sense, the president is the individual who is able to stir up the underlying current to achieve the turbulence necessary to propel policy from the status quo to a new equilibrium. Of course, the underlying current is composed of a number of factors that define the political context within which the president operates. In part, they represent institutional constraints (*Divided Government; Mandate; Advocacy*), and, in part, they represent opportunities for the discontinuous and evolutionary change that North (1990) describes (*Advocacy; House Liberalism; Senate Liberalism*).

In this study, the focus is on one salient issue area, national health care policy. In fact, domestic health care policy is an ideal topic because it is consistently in the top ten concerns of the American public according to Gallup public opinion data (Gallup, 2001; see also Table 1.1). Further, health care accounts for approximately 14% of the gross national product of the country. These two factors are undoubtedly the reason that changes in health care policy are frequently proposed and considered at the federal level, thereby making it a dynamic policy topic, amenable to policy change research.[2]

POLICY CHANGE RESEARCH

Much of the traditional policy change literature focuses on Congress (Kingdon, 1984; Wright, Rieselbach, & Dodd, 1986). Recent research (Jones, 1995; Schneider & Teske, with Mintrom, 1995) examines dynamic models that incorporate other actors at various levels of government. For example, Schneider and Teske with Mintrom (1995) identify and examine individuals they refer to as "entrepreneurs as agents for change." Recall that an entrepreneur is a politically motivated individual seeking to create dramatic policy changes. Thus, Schneider and Teske focus on the efforts of a single individual, creating the momentum for change in the various studies they present.

In contrast, other research focuses on interest groups and their role in policy change, arguing that an individual alone cannot move policy without the support of policy networks (Jenkins-Smith & Sabatier, 1993). Additionally, Baumgartner and Jones (1993) introduce the theory of destabilizing events, an area further discussed by Roberts and King (1996). In this theory, certain events destabilize the policy environment and create opportunities for dramatic change. Together, these authors have created a substantial body of research on policy change in the United States that is supported by empirical evidence.

While these works provide a picture of policy change, in general, the focus is either on local government (Schneider & Teske with Mintrom, 1995) or on the consequences of policy change (Baumgartner & Jones, 1993, p. 12). Hence, a gap in the literature emerges at the national level. Although it is acknowledged that the national-level policy entrepreneur brings about dynamic policy change (Baumgartner & Jones, 1993; Schiller, 1995), there has not been a formal quantitative examination of the role of the president as a policy entrepreneur. Nevertheless, the literature on policy entrepreneurs seems to describe the activity of the president in pursuing his policy goals. For example, entrepreneurs are said to engage in the pursuit of policy innovation (Kingdon, 1984; Polsby, 1984). They are also assumed to define and frame policy issues (Kingdon, 1984; Riker, 1986). Finally, they are thought to engage in networking (Kingdon, 1984; Smith, 1991) and coalition building (Eyestone, 1978; Smith, 1991). All of these activities are similar to the activities of a president in seeking legislation (see, for example, Neustadt, 1990). While these authors set out convincing arguments that the activities in which a president engages are like those of an entrepreneur, none go beyond that assertion and actually test whether there is evidence to support the hypothesis that the president is and can be a policy entrepreneur.

Other authors examine certain aspects of the policy change dynamic. For example, Carmines and Stimson (1986) introduce the theory of issue evolution. The authors argue that policy change occurs because of elite discourse that filters down to the public and then spurs the public to collectively advocate, at the grassroots level, for the policy change. This separates the public from purely institutional actors working through interest groups to individual-level actors who are influenced by elites and in turn influence elites. This complements the notion that policy entrepreneurs can transform policy issues that deserve debate into policy problems that require solutions (Baumgartner & Jones, 1993; Cobb & Elder, 1983; Hilgartner & Bosk, 1988).

While several authors mention the possible role of the president in dynamic policy change (Baumgartner & Jones, 1993; Carmines & Stimson, 1986; Conley, 2001; Edwards, 1983; Jones, 1995; Ragsdale, 1984, 1987; Schneider & Teske with Mintrom, 1995), none directly tests the role of the president in this process. Baumgartner and Jones (1993) come closest:

> One cannot understand the rise and decline of the national urban initiative without appreciating the particular confluence of factors that occurred during the 1960s. An unprecedented window of opportunity opened during that time in which three major social trends came into juxtaposition: America's post-war prosperity; social attitudes that, for a brief moment in history turned from economics to social issues; and a high watermark of the Democratic Rooseveltian coalition, led by an *activist president* [italics added] with an ambitious social agenda. (p. 144)

In this research, these theories are used to develop a model designed to test whether the president acts as a policy entrepreneur. The concept of an activist president is combined with the idea that the success or failure of a proposal to change policy is context dependent. By creating a unique model using an innovative estimation procedure that identifies contextual variables in the political environment that influence presidential action and the votes of members of Congress, it is possible to empirically understand what creates the "window of opportunity" described by Kingdon (1984) and Baumgartner and Jones (1993). The goal is to understand the conditions under which policy can and does change; that is, to understand how health care policy changes, within the prevailing path dependent system in play in the United States while keeping in mind the mediating effect of public opinion.

This exploration rests on critical assumptions that are based in existing literature. These include (1) the assumption that change can occur within a path dependent system (Baumgartner & Jones, 1993; North, 1990); (2) the assumption that presidents have policy preferences (Cameron, 2000; Conley, 2001; Jacobs & Shapiro, 2000); and (3) the assumption that presidents use their position to try to influence policy outcomes (Conley, 2001; Fett, 1992; Jacobs & Shapiro, 2000; Kernell, 1986). Taken together, these assumptions add to our understanding of why a president would pursue policy change. Of course, the question of when a president will pursue policy change and with what success is the focus of this chapter.

THE PRESIDENTS AND THEIR POLICIES

The idea that presidents pursue policies is not shocking—in fact, it is expected. In her book *Presidential Mandates* (2001), Patricia Heidotting Conley devotes a significant part of her analysis to explaining that while all presidents have policy preferences, only presidents who claim to have a mandate actually pursue those policies. By way of explaining this, Conley writes that those elections in which the president cannot claim a mandate and thus is unable to pursue his policy preferences are "not 'mandates for the status quo' because the [candidate] . . . did not win by opposing change. Rather, these elections failed to convey a signal for change . . . the status quo resulted by default rather than by design" (p. 166).

The importance of the signal for change in the success of entrepreneurial policy initiatives is a recurring theme. For example, Schneider and Teske with Mintrom (1995) note, "In political systems, radical change is often associated with the emergence of new leaders, the development of new political movements, and the introductions of new policies. Ideas and coalitions that appeared firmly entrenched and impervious to change are washed away more quickly than seemed possible" (p. 3). Thus, this would lead one to theorize that newly elected presidents serving in a time when the public desires change would be most successful. While this may be an accurate description of the broad environmental conditions necessary for policy change, whether change occurs depends on the political context.

One important element in the discussion of context is the concept of the presidential mandate. Conley explores this notion in depth, by identifying the type of mandate with the descriptions based upon presidential claims and media coverage following the election. The presidential elections covered in this chapter include "popular mandates" (1952, 1964, 1980), "bargained mandates" (1948, 1992), and "victories but not mandates" (1960, 1976, 1988). The concept of a mandate is very important to understanding whether a president can and will pursue policy change. Recall that the theory of policy change within a path dependent system is contingent on there being enough turbulence within a policy area to open the window of opportunity and propel the policy change that the president is seeking through it. This is important to the present study in that Conley identifies election issues that defined the mandates. In two cases, health care was a defining issue (1964, 1992). In 1964, an election that Conley identifies as a "popular mandate," President Johnson had his Medicare proposal pending. In fact, in October 1964, Johnson acknowledged that the election could determine the fate of Medicare: "I think Senator Gore very properly presented the situation when he said that it is now a matter that the people of this country can pass judgment on. I hope we get a mandate in November." The other is President Clinton's "bargained mandate" in 1992. In that case, the Health Security Act that ultimately emerged in September 1993 was the issue and the mandate was bargained because, although the Democrats held both houses of Congress, Clinton had been elected with only a plurality of the vote (Conley, 2001).

Other important components of the political context in which the president governs have been examined before. For example, in Peterson's (1990) work, considering the context of presidential activity is of great importance in improving understanding:

> Presidential proposals are not considered in a political vacuum; the actions of both the president and the members of Congress as a whole are influenced, one may presume, by a diversity of factors that establish the specific contexts in which the decisions are concluded. The characteristics of the decision setting for each proposal shape the incentives of each participant in the process by adjusting around the margins the costs and benefits of particular courses of action as they are perceived by the participants. (p. 89)

Fett (1992) supports the importance of the role of context in his examination of the possibility of strategic behavior by the president in achieving his agenda. Fett concluded that presidents do not act strategically; rather, they reveal their true legislative agendas. These agendas are tempered only by what they think they can achieve given the political context in which they find themselves.

This is an idea that is also addressed in Cameron's (2000) examination of the negative power of the presidents through vetoes. While Cameron's focus is on the president as a block to legislation through the use of the veto, in contrast to the present study where the president is treated as the moving party in legislative proposals, the discussions are, in fact, complementary. Early in his book, Cameron notes that "there are three ways vetoes can shape legislation. First, an intransigent president can try to kill a bill. . . . [S]econd, the president can force Congress to craft a new, veto-proof version of the bill. . . . [T]hird, the president can force Congress to rewrite the vetoed bill" (p. 20). In this sense, Cameron is describing, in part, the context within which Congress operates. Likewise, when the president is the main proponent of legislation, he faces the inherent veto powers that Congress possesses. Like the presidential veto, Congress can use its powers at various stages to reshape the president's policy initiatives: Congress can simply refuse to consider the proposal—that is, not allow a version of the president's policy to be introduced onto the floor—or, should the president find a congressional ally willing to introduce the legislation, allow it to die in committee. However, if the legislation makes it to the floor, it can be rejected by a majority. Thus, Congress has at its disposal as many methods to confound the president's agenda as it does to promote the president's agenda. This, like the veto power of the president, is a part of the context in which decisions take place.

Defining Context

To define the context, it is necessary to observe the political variables that define the power and motivations of actors in the political environment, as well as the variables that define the attitudes of the actors within that environment. Together, these should effectively model the characteristics of the environment within which the decision is made. However, the task is to identify those things that define the context.

Conley's (2001) discussion of the context in which presidents pursue policy change goes far in helping identify the necessary elements to model the process of presidents pursuing policy change within a path dependent system:

> Presidents would like to change the policy agenda to bring it more in line with their own preferences, but they do not have an incentive to make changes if they believe they will fail. The congressional response to the president's agenda depends upon: (1) beliefs about public support for the president's program; (2) the proximity of the president's policy position to that of members of Congress; and (3) the relationship of both to the status quo. Elections supply the data necessary for the president's calculations. . . . Elections also send signals to elected officials about the strength of support for the president's policy agenda. A president claims a mandate when the election signals strong support for his agenda. (p. 6)

In this passage, Conley identifies the parameters of a model for studying presidential policy initiatives. First, there is the decision of whether to pursue policy change at all (*Proposed*), thus a critical variable is the attitude of the president (*Presidential Liberalism*). For example, one would expect that as a president's own preferences are more liberal, he would be more likely to propose liberal policy changes. Moreover, the actions of the president are constrained by the other actors, which also define the window of opportunity for policy change (*Advocacy*). For example, as Conley alludes, one would expect the attitudes and partisanship of the Congress to be important because the president cannot directly introduce legislation (*Divided Government; House Liberalism; Senate Liberalism*). Of course, the actions of the Congress are, in turn, constrained by the public's mood and preferences (*Health Policy Attitude; Climate; Presidential Popularity; Mandate*) (Kingdon, 1989; Schiller, 1995).

Modeling the role of the public is important because of the impact the public has on members of Congress. For example, Kingdon's (1989) research indicates that members of Congress get their primary voting cues from their constituents. Moving from the individual level to the aggregate level, one can conceptualize the role of the public simply as general attitudes toward the policy area or toward the size of government in general (Stimson, 1999). One can also model the public attitude toward the president in terms of popularity, which Mueller (1970) describes as "a general impression about the way the incumbent seems to be handling his job at the present moment" (p. 18). Finally, there is the notion of policy destabilization due to the advocacy efforts of interest groups (Baumgartner & Jones, 1993), which makes policy issues more salient (McCarthy, McPhail, & Smith, 1996) and thereby adds to attitude formation by the public (Zaller, 1992).[3]

However, to define political context attitudes, there is a need for a greater level of theoretical justification. The theory that attitudes of the elites—that is, the president and the members of Congress—are important to policy formation is widely accepted (McClosky & Zaller, 1984). Nevertheless, individual elite attitudes are tempered to some extent by the actions and beliefs of the public at large. For example, McClosky and Zaller (1984) note that "the capacity of leaders to influence public opinion is obviously limited—though it is difficult to say to what degree and under what circumstances. Leaders are aware of this limitation and are usually reluctant to push policies that depart too far from the attitudes of the electorate" (p. 153). Further, as Kingdon (1989) notes, "It is likely that constituency imposes some meaningful constraints on Congressmen's voting behavior" (p. 68). Thus, it would seem that controlling for both the mood of the public and the attitudes of political elites is a necessary part of any meaningful model of the policy process. Page and Shapiro (1992) support this notion: "On an issue he cares about, a president can hammer away with repeated speeches and statements and can expect to achieve a 5 or 10 percentage point change in public opinion over the course of several months. . . . Moreover, he can probably exert additional (indirect) influence upon the public by persuading other opinion leaders to take similar stands" (p. 349). Following Page and Shapiro, the president must look to whether the public is receptive enough to the change that they can be persuaded to support him.

Of course, the constraints are just one facet of the equation. Other important factors in defining the political context lie in the ability of the president to persuade (Neustadt, 1990). This, it would seem, depends on the president's ability to persuade not only the members of Congress but also the public. These considerations enter into the decision calculus of the president when considering whether to make a policy proposal (Conley, 2001; Neustadt, 1990). Thus, one would assume that the president relies on his intuition about the strength and stability of his coalition in Congress, members of which will be requested to introduce his legislation. Further, the president oftentimes reacts to observable advocacy efforts (Jacobs & Shapiro, 2000; McCarthy, McPhail, & Smith, 1996).

Similar factors determine whether the policy, once proposed, will be passed into law. For example, the public mood and the partisanship of the Congress should influence the outcome of the proposal. Other variables may also emerge as important. One of these is presidential popularity, which Mueller (1970) broadly defines as a vote of confidence in the president. However, the value of this measure as an indicator of presidential influence is an area of contention. For example, Bond and Fleisher (1990) argue that, overall, presidential popularity has little, if any, impact on presidential success in Congress. Nevertheless, the authors do use the presidential popularity measure as a predictor variable in their model. The Bond and Fleisher finding of limited impact for presidential popularity as a predictor of policy success is supported, to some extent, by Edwards (1989).

The notion central to this research is the ability of the president to lead public opinion and thus achieve policy change. That the popularity of the president plays a role is well established. In addition to the discussed literature, a wealth of research suggests that popular presidents can sway public opinion (Edwards, 1983; Kernell, 1993; Mondak, 1993; Page & Shapiro, 1984; Page, Shapiro, & Dempsey, 1987; Rosen, 1973; Sigelman, 1980; Thomas & Bass, 1982; Thomas & Sigelman, 1985). Some evidence supports the notion that unpopular presidents can actually reduce public support for programs that they are advocating (Sigelman & Sigelman, 1981). Cohen (1995) combines the research of MacKuen (1983) and the presidential popularity theorists, demonstrating that presidents, through speeches, can indirectly persuade opinions by bringing the issue to the attention of the public. (But see Jacobs and Shapiro, 2000, for a contrary finding.) Popular presidents accomplish this because people are more likely to be receptive to messages from that source. Thus, the power to persuade is entwined with popularity.

Several authors examine presidential popularity as an indicator of probable success. Most recently, Brace and Hinckley (1992) found that presidential popularity affects votes in the legislature. This is a finding supported by Ostrom and Simon (1985) and Rivers and Rose (1985). Further impact is suggested by Page and Shapiro (1992), who note that when presidential popularity is high, elites generally fall into lock step behind the president. This is tempered by the limited possibility of a nonrecursive or reciprocal relationship between presidential action and public opinion; that is, that presidential actions influence public opinion even as public opinion is influencing presidential action. Page and Shapiro also found "in scrutinizing specific cases . . . some indications that the relationship between presidents (actions) and public opinion is, indeed, reciprocal with each influencing the other" (p. 349). Further, Edwards, Mitchell, and Welch (1995) show that presidential action on highly salient issues, as reported by the media, directly influences presidential popularity. MacKuen (1983) suggests a method for increasing popularity identifying short-term boosts associated with presidential speeches and foreign travel. Thus, although the relationship is small, there does appear to be some feedback from efforts at persuasion and presidential popularity, which is one of the tools of persuasion. However, in all cases, the main effect on policy change is popularity driven (see also Ragsdale, 1984, 1987; Edwards, 1983.)

Sullivan (1991a) investigates the existence of declining presidential influence over the course of the president's term. The theory asserts that the president begins with high popularity and a great level of support for his agenda. This concept is similar to the coalition of minorities argument asserted by Mueller (1970) which states that the electorate gives presidents only a short-lived mandate. Thus, any attempts at policy change must be swift, before both public and congressional support erodes. Sullivan (1991a) finds the most conclusive evidence for the "bank account" model in the Johnson administration, where the 16 million–vote mandate over Barry Goldwater rapidly dissipated during his term. Johnson, as quoted by Sullivan, recognized a half-life for this effect: "I've just been elected and right now we'll have a honeymoon with Congress. . . . I'll have a good chance of getting my program through. But after I make my recommendations, I'm going to start to lose the power and authority I have. . . . [E]very day that I'm in office and every day that I push my program, I'll be losing part of my ability to be influential" (pp. 686–687). Thus, one would be wise to control for this mandate phenomenon, recognized not only by President Johnson, but also by Conley (2001), Mueller (1970), and Sullivan (1991a).

Further, there is the specter of divided government. This is touched on somewhat by taking into account the partisan and ideological composition of the Congress as well as the partisanship and ideology of the president. Although Mayhew (1991) has found that there is little direct support for the notion that unified governments are more productive, divided government is nevertheless a factor for which there should be some form of control.

In summary, the political context within which a president acts as an agent for policy change and his success as an agent is defined by several measures: first, by the public, making its preference known in a measurable sense through its receptiveness to change; second, by the Congress, with loyalty to both party leadership and their constituents; and third, by the popularity of the president and by the circumstances surrounding the president's election. To achieve success, it seems that the president must be cognizant of these constraints when proposing a policy change. He must recognize, as Johnson did, when the political environment will favor policy change. However, the president can also act as a force for change by pushing at the parameters of the context, stirring the debate as it were. As Page and Shapiro (1992), Cohen (1995), and MacKuen (1983) show, the president can move public opinion, even slightly, toward favoring his program, an important effect at the margins, given a mediating influence of public opinion. Fett's (1994) research supports this notion in his study showing effects for the interaction of presidential popularity and presidential advocacy in the House during President Ronald Reagan's first year in office. In short, the past research points to an interactive relationship between the president, Congress, and the public in regard to policy change. In this study, I test this hypothesis in the realm of health care policy.

A Brief History of Presidential Health Policy Initiatives

To examine the context in which a president advocates national health policy change, it is necessary to understand the political environment in which the decisions of whether to propose policy initiatives are made. For that reason, a review of the major presidential initiatives in national health care is in order. The line of reasoning begins with a discussion of presidential involvement with health policy change during the term of Franklin Roosevelt, when federal intervention into health care, through the establishment of a national health insurance plan, first became a subject of presidential advocacy.

President Roosevelt established the Committee on Economic Security, led by Frances Perkins, the secretary of labor, to design a social insurance system for the United States based on those in place in western Europe. The committee recommended inclusion of a national health insurance program, funded by a 1% payroll tax, within the Social Security program. While the Social Security Act sent to Congress by President Roosevelt in 1935 included this provision, the president quickly sacrificed it in the negotiations with Congress. President Roosevelt's next revision of the Social Security Act, in 1939, included a request for national health insurance that the White House again quickly dropped, realizing that the dominant health policy attitudes were conservative (Koff & Park, 1999; Schottland, 1963).

During World War II, health care changed dramatically because of technological advances and new methods of financing health care. The country emerged from the war with a new health insurance system that more closely resembled a market and with a new president, Harry Truman. Attitudes of the public and the elites toward health care were clustered at the more conservative end of the spectrum.

Despite this political environment, President Truman was perhaps the most vociferous advocate for national health insurance ever to occupy the White House, repeatedly calling for national health insurance during his tenure. In fact, he truly represents Page and Shapiro's (1992) model of a president trying to advance his policy goals by "hammering away" at his program. However, despite his energetic advocacy, he was unable to realize his goal of national health insurance during his term in office (McCullough, 1992).

Explaining the defeats of Roosevelt and Truman is possible using the contextual argument, I have presented. The economic collapse caused by the Great Depression coincided with a liberal shift in public attitudes and, for that reason, despite opposition from powerful members of Congress and the Supreme Court, the New Deal was enacted. However, at that time, the federal provision of health care was not a major concern, thus national health insurance was not achieved. In terms of the process discussed earlier, while the attitudes of the president and the Congress were prepared for liberal policy change, public attitudes toward health policy were much more conservative than public attitudes toward other areas of social policy. Further, the advocacy for health care reform was not present, as it had been for Social Security and depression relief. Thus, President Roosevelt withdrew his proposal for national health insurance (Skocpol, 1995).

By 1946, not only had the United States entered a conservative era that inhibited progressive change, but also the health insurance system switched to one in which private commercial insurers offered inexpensive plans to the public (McCullough, 1992; Skocpol, 1995). There was no need for the government to become involved. While this context did not hinder President Truman from proposing a change, it did preclude passage. Truman struggled with his popularity ratings and used much of his political capital in his battles with General Douglas MacArthur and the steel producers. Further, Truman faced an increasingly conservative populace and a Republican Congress for much of his time as president (McCullough, 1992; Neustadt, 1990).

In 1955, the state of health care in the United States changed. After years of culling the lowest risk groups from community rating systems[4] only the old and the sick were left in the community insurance pools. The community-rated premiums soared and the enrollees dropped out, becoming uninsured. While the Eisenhower administration maintained the status quo in federal health care policy, at this time the provision of health benefits was seen primarily as an employer responsibility. This created the era of powerful commercial insurance companies who engaged in a practice of "cherry picking," that is, writing low premium insurance contracts for the healthiest members of the population. The system used to determine premiums became age sensitive, while insurance became increasingly tied to employment. These combined to create a crisis in the late 1950s and early 1960s as millions of elderly and indigent citizens were denied health care because of their inability to afford health insurance (Feldstein, 1993; Marmor, 1994; Skocpol, 1995). One proposed solution was the Kerr–Mills plan introduced in 1960 as an alternative to a national health system for the elderly (see Mayhew, 1991). Although this plan enjoyed at least tacit support from President Dwight Eisenhower (Schottland, 1963), and ultimately passed, it did not completely address the problems of the increasing number of uninsured elderly (Koff & Park, 1996).

The crisis combined with the liberal mood sweeping the country, and culminated in 1965, after years of advocacy by both President John Kennedy and President Lyndon Johnson, in the Medicare and Medicaid Acts. These programs were designed to provide government-financed health insurance to the elderly and indigent. They also represented the first real attempt at providing health care by the federal government (Marmor, 1994; Skocpol, 1995).

In the early 1970s, as the country turned more conservative, President Richard Nixon proposed a conservative health care plan, the Health Maintenance Organization Act. This policy was designed to control rising costs in health care by establishing integrated prepaid insurance plans (Brown, 1983; see also Marmor, 1994). Recall that if policy initiatives are context dependent, then it is logical that conservative periods such as the Nixon years result in the success of conservative plans, while in liberal periods, liberal plans should succeed.

For much of the next two decades, despite presidential advocacy (see Table 4.1 on page 54), it seemed that the federal role in the provision of health care was resolved, with the brief exception of the ill-fated federal foray into catastrophic health care coverage; the federal agenda was the maintenance of Medicare and Medicaid and a laissez-faire approach in all other areas. However, in 1992, with roughly 40 million Americans uninsured, President Clinton was elected, promising to provide universal access to health care for all Americans. The president established a commission, headed by First Lady Hillary Clinton, to assess the state of health care and to develop a national health care policy within the first 100 days of the Clinton administration. Public opinion polls indicated that the mood of the country had shifted to one favoring the public provision of health insurance and it seemed that national health insurance was a certainty.

The commission was delayed in preparing the legislation and it was not until October 1993 that President Clinton went before Congress to introduce the Health Security Act. The act was forwarded to the Congressional committees where intensive hearings were held for the next nine months. Ultimately, like Truman's national health care plan, nearly 50 years earlier, Clinton's Health Security Act failed. The question examined in the following analysis is What factors contributed to the failures of Clinton and Truman and the success of Johnson?

The explanation lies as much with the president as it does with the public. Indeed, as Page and Shapiro (1992) write, "*[P]opular presidents* [italics added] were estimated to have a significant effect on opinion, while unpopular presidents had no impact" (p. 349). Further, they argue that "the estimated impact of popular presidents probably reflects a reciprocal relationship, in which popularity-seeking presidents take a stand in response to public opinion or in anticipation of it" (p. 349). Thus, in that sense, the president can act in true entrepreneurial fashion by not only seizing an opportunity (high popularity), but also by using it to mold the political environment. This phenomenon is most important in the proposal phase, and is captured by a variable modeling a presidential mandate.

DATA AND METHODS

Recall that the primary objective in this chapter is to examine the political context—the nature—of the underlying turbulence in the policy system in which a president proposes a policy and the political factors that contribute to the success or failure of that policy. This examination suggests a two-stage selection equation, for two reasons. First, there is an underlying interest in modeling the relationship between a president proposing a health policy initiative and the contextual variables that could predict such an event. Second, there is a desire to understand the relationship between the policy, once proposed, being approved by Congress and another set of contextual variables that predict passage. The two are, of course, related in that the first event—the proposal—affects the second—the approval. This is so because Congress cannot approve policies not proposed.[5] Thus, the situation presents a classic selection bias model (Achen, 1986; Hanushek & Jackson, 1977). The best way to model this relationship is through the use of a selection equation (4.1) for the proposal of the presidential policy and an outcome equation (4.2) predicting approval. Keeping in mind King's (1993) admonition that we seek to model the process generating our observations, rather than the observations themselves, the following model is suggested:

Proposed = β_0 + β_1 House Liberalism + β_2 Senate Liberalism +
$\quad$ β_3 Presidential Liberalism + β_4 Mandate + β_5 Advocacy +
$\quad$ β_6 Health Policy Attitude + ϵ $\qquad$ (4.1)

Policy Approved = β_0 + β_1 Presidential Popularity + β_2 Senate Liberalism +
$\quad$ β_3 House Liberalism + β_4 Mandate + β_5 Climate +
$\quad$ β_6 Divided Government + β_7 Hazard Rate +
$\quad$ β_8 Residuals + ϵ $\qquad$ (4.2)

(For a complete discussion of the methodological aspects of this analysis, please see the Methodological Appendix.)

Expectations

As mentioned earlier, the variables included in the model are driven by the existing theory in the literature. Overall, the model is designed to build on this research, while integrating the theories to create a greater understanding of the role of the president, the Congress, and the public in the process that leads to the precipice of policy change. That is, the model is designed to shed some light on how or under what conditions health policy can make the evolutionary leap that carries it beyond the path dependent outcome that one would predict devoid of other information.

Based on past research, the selection equation variables are designed to represent factors that influence the likelihood that a president will propose a change in policy. Health policy attitudes of the electorate toward various policy initiatives is always a concern for politicians with an eye toward reelection (Fenno, 1978; Mayhew, 1974; McCullough, 1992). Further, as Kingdon (1984) notes, "People in and around government sense a national mood . . . [that] changes from one time to another in discernable ways, and that these changes in mood or climate have important impacts on policy agendas and policy outcomes" (p. 153). Thus, public mood should be a good predictor of the likelihood of a president proposing a policy.

In addition, liberalism variables for the president, the House, and the Senate should be good predictors of the likelihood that a president will propose a liberal policy change and that Congress will adopt the change, thus these variables are expected to emerge as significant predictors in both equations. Finally, advocacy and mandate will provide more power to the estimation; one would not expect them to be substantial predictors in the selection equation.

Nevertheless, advocacy must be included for two reasons: First, as Baumgartner and Jones (1993) note, advocacy efforts can destabilize the policy environment enough to allow for policy change (see also Roberts & King, 1996; Schneider & Teske, with Mintrom, 1995.) Second, although the explanation for this is based in media studies beyond the scope of this paper, advocacy can make an issue salient to the president and the public, thereby making the president more likely to propose a policy change (MacKuen, 1983; McCarthy, McPhail, & Smith, 1996).

Together, these variables should predict the likelihood of a president proposing a liberal policy change in health care, a crucial component of the selection model. The outcome equation is of greater interest in that it models the relationship between the president, the Congress, and the public. Here the interest lies in modeling the likelihood of a presidential health policy initiative being approved by Congress. That is, given that the president reaches into the turbulence underlying American health care policy and determines that the conditions are ripe for an evolutionary change, what is the likelihood that the change will occur?

The expectation is that the power, or perceived power, of the president is an important factor in the voting decisions of the members of Congress (Kingdon, 1989). Thus, presidential popularity should exert a major influence on the likelihood that a policy will pass (Conley, 2001). Recall that presidential popularity is a measure of nothing less than how well the president's message resonates with the public. This is the public who will vote in the next election for or against the entire House of Representatives and one third of the senators who are deciding the fate of the president's policy initiative. Further, presidential popularity provides a proxy measure for presidential influence. Thus, there is an expectation that presidential popularity will positively correlate with the outcome of the vote. However, plummeting popularity can have dire consequences on a president's policy initiatives.

While presidential popularity is theoretically exogenous to the Congress, it may influence the voting decisions of the members of Congress. However, given that presidential popularity arises with the public, not the Congress, it fails to capture the full complement of variables that enter into the voting decision of a member of Congress. Thus, a simple measure of the responsiveness of the Congress to liberal policy change is used: the attitudes or liberalism of the members of Congress captured in the House Liberalism and Senate Liberalism measures used in the selection equation. This usage is based in the theory that elites, like the general public, follow certain health policy metaphors that can be captured by their ideological attitudes. Liberals on the whole should be more amenable to approving federal interventions in the provision of health care, given that countless liberal platforms have included calls for national health insurance. Further, noted liberals, such as Senators Ted Kennedy, Harris Wofford, and Paul Wellstone have been closely associated with national health policy legislation. Finally, the three major initiatives (Truman's plan, Medicare and Medicaid, and the Health Security Act) were liberal proposals. (For a complete list of health policy proposals and initiatives and the presidents associated with them, please see Table 4.1.)

Climate should be both substantively and statistically significant as a predictor of policy approval. Thomas and Pika (1997) remark that, "the national mood is, then, a reflection of the politically relevant climate or temper of the times" (p. 335). This observation, along with theories discussed earlier, supports the importance of public attitudes as one of the constraints on policy approval. For this reason one would expect that the mood of the public, which is nothing more than the public attitude toward the size of government, will have a substantial positive impact on the likelihood that a liberal presidential proposal will succeed.

Finally, Divided Government becomes important in that the question of what impact this situation has on policy change is unsettled. During the period covered in this study, 22 of the 44 years have been periods of divided government

TABLE 4.1

Presidential Health Policy Proposals Compiled from the Papers of the Presidents

President	Policy	Outcome*
Eisenhower	Kerr–Mills Grant Proposal (alternative to federal health insurance for the elderly)	Passed 1960
Kennedy	Medicare	Failed
	Migrant Health Act (clinics for migrant farm workers)	Passed 1962
	Aid for Mentally Ill and Retarded	Passed 1963
	Aid to Medical Schools	Passed 1963
Johnson	Medicare Federally Financed Health Insurance for the Elderly	Passed 1965
	Medicaid Federal- and State-Financed Health Insurance for Indigents	Passed 1965
Nixon	National Cancer Act	Passed 1971
	Health Maintenance Organization Act	Passed 1973
Ford	National Health Planning and Resources Development Act (tacit presidential support)	Passed 1974
Carter	National Health Insurance	Failed
Reagan	Catastrophic Health Insurance for the Aged	Passed 1988 (Repealed 1989)
Bush	Medicaid Extension to Cover Uninsured	Failed
Clinton	Health Security Act	Failed
	Medicaid Extension to Cover Uninsured Children (SCHIP)	Passed 1997
	Patient's Bill of Rights	Passed 2003

Source: Compiled from *Congressional Quarterly Almanac.*

(where at least one house of the legislature was controlled by the party in opposition to the president). Whether this is important remains in question. In one corner, Mayhew (1991) concludes, "Surprisingly, it does not seem to make all that much difference whether party control of the American government happens to be unified or divided" (p. 198). However, Cameron (2000) argues that it is indeed an important component of presidential politics: "During divided government the president and Congress frequently find themselves at loggerheads over legislation. In the system constructed by the Founders, the president's principal legislative tool is the veto and he has every incentive to use it in a struggle with Congress over policy" (p. 25). Thus, relying on Mayhew's assessment, it may be easy to immediately expect that there should be no influence from modeling divided government; that is, the coefficient for a divided government model should be insignificant. However, if Cameron is correct, then one would expect to see an effect, unless of course divided government, an easily identifiable situation, is already within the president's decision calculus. If that were the case, then we would expect that Divided Government would be insignificant as well.

Before discussing the analysis it is useful to view the basic statistics for the variables to enable a better understanding of the data (see Table 4.2). One of the interesting items is the narrow range of liberalism in both the House and the Senate. Further, as the reader will note, there were 58 quarters in which the president made a liberal health policy proposal, counting all opportunities ranging from campaign speeches to the State of the Union Address over the 172 quarters studied. During 10 of these quarters, liberal policy changes were approved. These ranged from extensions of programs to the Medicare and

TABLE 4.2
Frequencies of the Variables ($N = 172$)

Variable	Mean	Standard Error of the Mean	Minimum	Maximum
Proposed	0.34	0.04	0.00	1.00
Approved	0.06	0.02	0.00	1.00
House Liberalism	0.70	0.09	0.45	0.85
Senate Liberalism	0.60	0.12	0.16	0.84
Presidential Liberalism	0.40	0.12	0.21	0.67
Health Policy Attitude	0.84	0.01	0.57	1.00
Advocacy	0.34	0.19	−4.00	4.00
Presidential Popularity	0.55	0.92	0.24	0.83
Climate	0.58	0.01	0.47	0.70
Mandate	0.37	0.02	0.07	0.98

Medicaid Acts. (For more detail regarding coding and criteria, please see the Methodological Appendix.)

The system of equations (4.1 and 4.2) was analyzed using a two-stage-conditional maximum likelihood approach due to the dichotomous nature of the dependent variable in the outcome equation (Alvarez, 1994; Maddala, 1983; Rivers & Vuong, 1988). This approach is generally superior to linear probability models that typically yield attenuated estimates of the standard errors of the coefficients because of the heteroscedastic nature of the error term and the correlation across equations of the errors (Alvarez, 1994; Rivers & Vuong, 1988). Probit is used to estimate both equations because of the assumption of a normal distribution and the need to match the distributional assumptions across equations.

RESULTS

Table 4.3 presents the results for the estimation of the selection equation. As expected, with the exception of the House Liberalism parameter estimate, the liberalism variables are significant positive predictors of the likelihood that a president will make a liberal policy proposal. One possible explanation for the failure of the House variable is statistical, in that there is probably a high level of multicollinearity with the Senate variable. However, to exclude either of the two congressional variables would lead to model misspecification and would introduce an element of bias into the model. Another explanation is the possibility that when the Congress is liberal, the president is less likely to propose liberal health policy change. At first, this seems counterintuitive. However, if one considers this in terms of the political process, it is logical that the president would allow health policy initiatives to be "floated" in the House, jumping on the bandwagon if they are popular and ignoring them if they are not, thereby avoiding associations with failed policies (see chapter 7) and taking credit for successful policies (Fett, 1992, 1994; Peterson, 1990).

Health Policy Attitude, the variable modeling public attitudes toward liberal health policy initiatives, is a strong predictor of the likelihood that the president will propose such a policy. For example, moving across the range of Health Policy Attitude, in the liberal direction, results in an increased likelihood of approximately 56% that the president will propose a liberal change in health policy, holding the other variables at their minimum. (Recall that I define a liberal change as a greater role for government in the provision of health care.)

This would seem to be a clear indication that the president operates as an entrepreneur, recognizing when the political conditions are most receptive to a liberal policy change. The president takes advantage of these conditions in the political environment to propose his dynamic policy change, much as a policy entrepreneur would. This harkens back to the concept of a nonrecursive rela-

TABLE 4.3

Selection Equation (Proposed as Dependent) ($N = 172$)

	β	SE
House Liberalism	−0.042***	0.112
Senate Liberalism	0.29**	0.111
Presidential Liberalism	0.31***	0.009
Mandate	0.29	0.422
Advocacy	0.01	0.132
Health Policy Attitude	3.11**	1.212
Constant	−3.31**	1.203
Log Likelihood = −86.646		
Chi^2 = 46.58		

**$p < .05$;   ***$p < .001$.

TABLE 4.4

Two-Stage-Conditional-Maximum-Likelihood Estimates
(Policy Approved as Dependent Variable) ($N = 172$)

	β	SE
Presidential Popularity	8.450**	3.360
Senate Liberalism	0.056*	0.033
House Liberalism	−0.054*	0.039
Mandate	2.467**	1.248
Climate	20.647**	10.510
Divided Government	0.289	0.744
Hazard Rate	0.658***	0.230
Residuals	−1.524	7.210
Constant	−24.182**	13.493
Log Likelihood = −23.106		
Chi^2 = 37.99		

*$p < .10$.   **$p < .05$.   ***$p < .001$

tionship between the president's ability to persuade and the public's willingness to support a policy. Of course, this idea of reciprocal causation must be tempered by the fact that it seems only to exist under specific circumstances: when both issue salience and presidential popularity are high (Page & Shapiro, 1992).

Table 4.4 presents the results of the outcome equation. In terms of policy change, the outcome equation is more significant, if not more interesting, in that it models the factors that determine whether an entrepreneurial president will be successful in achieving the dynamic policy change that he proposed. The nonsignificant coefficient estimate for the error term (residuals) suggests that the error correction procedure was successful (Rivers & Vuong, 1988). The true story emerges in the Presidential Popularity and Climate parameter estimates. Not only are these coefficients statistically significant, substantively they have enormous impact. This is much as the theory predicted and provides support for the notion that the key context variables Presidential Popularity and Climate are essential for moving policy. For example, on average, holding all other variables at their mean, a 10-point decline in Presidential Popularity results in a decreased likelihood of passage of a policy of approximately 1.5%. The effect for Climate is approximately a 4% increased likelihood of passage for a 10-point move in the liberal direction.

Overall, the model performed as expected. For example, Mandate has a significant impact on the likelihood of approval of a presidential policy initiative, much as theory and existing research (Conley, 2001) predicted. The liberalism of both the House and the Senate are not substantively significant predictors of the likelihood of a presidential health policy initiative being approved, nevertheless, they are important as control variables. They exhibit the same pattern as in the selection equation, with House Liberalism as a negative influence on policy approval. Again, one could argue statistically that this is a problem arising from multicollinearity. In the alternative, a possible explanation is that Congress is more beholden to special interests such as the American Medical Association and the National Health Insurance Institute and are less likely to support the nationalized health care opposed by these groups (Mazmanian & Sabatier, 1980). Substantively, these findings become more interesting through an examination of how these influences affected President Johnson's Medicare and Medicaid plan as well as Clinton's Health Security Act presented later in this chapter.

Finally, a discussion of divided government is needed. In the present model, Divided Government is not important. In fact, the standard error for the variable is nearly three times the coefficient. Thus, it would seem on the face that when it comes to presidential policy initiatives, Mayhew (1991) is correct: Divided government does not play a role. In contrast, Cameron (2000) lays out a complex model of presidential decision making in the context of the veto power of the president. In that model, divided government is an important factor that a president must weigh when considering whether to veto a policy that has either been introduced or passed entirely in the legislature, or that represents an altered version of a policy preferred by the president. Thus, there is equally compelling evidence that divided government should play a role (Cameron, 2000; Conley, 2001). As a result, the question is why it does not. One possibility, alluded to earlier, is that the impact of divided government is itself captured in the present model at a time before the president proposes the policy change. In that scenario, the president's decision whether to propose a change in policy is, at least in part, predicated on the presence or absence of a legislature in opposition.

DISCUSSION

Table 4.5 and Table 4.6 show the probability based on the selection equation, that the president would make the liberal health policy change proposal. These equations were analyzed for the periods surrounding the proposal of Medicare and Medicaid (Table 4.5) and the proposal of the Health Security Act (Table 4.6). In both analyses, the focus is on four variables of interest, the liberalism measures for the House, the Senate, and the president and the Health Policy Attitude of the public, varying their values to represent real-world conditions, while holding all other variables at their minimum. Together, these variables best define the context of the decision setting that the president faces when deciding whether to propose a policy change.

Table 4.5 shows the results for Medicare and Medicaid. President Johnson advocated this program while running for president in 1964. He formally proposed the Medicare and Medicaid plans after becoming president in his own right, taking advantage of the opportunity for policy change, rather than creating one. As one can see from scanning the table, the context, a liberal mood among the public, coupled with the liberal Congress and the liberal president make proposal overwhelmingly likely, with an increased likelihood of proposal that remains around 90%, holding all other variables at minimum.

TABLE 4.5

The Probability of Johnson Proposing Medicare and Medicaid from 1964 to 1965

Year and Quarter	Senate Liberalism	House Liberalism	Presidential Liberalism	Health Policy Attitude	Likelihood
1963 qtr. 4	84%	73%	65%	90%	85%
1964 qtr. 1	84%	73%	65%	98%	91%
1964 qtr. 2	84%	73%	65%	98%	91%
1964 qtr. 3	84%	73%	65%	98%	91%
1964 qtr. 4	80%	76%	67%	98%	91%
1965 qtr. 1	80%	76%	67%	97%	90%
1965 qtr. 2	80%	76%	67%	97%	90%
1965 qtr. 3	80%	76%	67%	97%	90%

TABLE 4.6
The Probability of Clinton Proposing the Health Security Act from 1993 to 1994

Year and Quarter	Senate Liberalism	House Liberalism	Presidential Liberalism	Health Policy Attitude	Likelihood
1993 qtr. 1	77%	62%	54%	88%	79%
1993 qtr. 2	77%	62%	54%	87%	78%
1993 qtr. 3	77%	62%	54%	87%	66%
1993 qtr. 4	77%	62%	54%	87%	66%
1994 qtr. 1	75%	61%	54%	86%	66%
1994 qtr. 2	75%	61%	54%	86%	66%
1994 qtr. 3	75%	61%	54%	85%	65%

In contrast, Table 4.6 shows how dramatically the likelihood of proposal is changed by context—in this case the context of the Clinton administration. Across the board, ranging from public mood to the president, the climate was much more conservative. While the increased likelihood of the president proposing a liberal policy change is about 70%, it is not as overwhelming as it was during the Medicare and Medicaid decision. This was probably reflected best by the Clinton administration's reticence to propose the Health Security Act. Thus, it would seem that context as measured in this model is a good predictor of policy proposal. Modeling other periods, such as the Carter or Reagan administration, one can see that the likelihood of proposal is exceedingly small and in fact the record reflects this with Carter's lackluster national health insurance proposal and Reagan's silence on the issue, with the notable exception of catastrophic health care late in his second term.

Table 4.7 and Table 4.8 show the substantive implications of this model, using the adoption of President Johnson's Medicare and Medicaid proposal and President Clinton's Health Security Act. Table 4.7 is the story of the success of Medicare and Medicaid with a popular president, a liberal majority in both Houses of Congress, a liberal climate, and a strong mandate. This, coupled with the fact that President Johnson took advantage of his first State of the Union Address following his landslide victory over Goldwater in 1964 to propose Medicare and Medicaid to Congress, points to a picture of success. As Table 4.7 shows, when Johnson proposed this health policy change, the political context assured victory. Even by the time it was brought to a vote during the second quarter of 1965, the increased likelihood was more than 71% that the measure would pass, taking into account the contextual variables. Thus, Johnson, a highly popular president, with an impressive mandate, was able to achieve the policy change that he desired.

TABLE 4.7

The Probability of Medicare and Medicaid Passing from 1964 to 1965

Year and Quarter	Presidential Popularity	Senate Liberalism	House Liberalism	Climate	Mandate	Likelihood
1963 qtr. 4	76%	84%	73%	58%	90%	76%
1964 qtr. 1	76%	84%	73%	58%	45%	76%
1964 qtr. 2	74%	84%	73%	58%	23%	72%
1964 qtr. 3	70%	84%	73%	61%	12%	72%
1964 qtr. 4	68%	80%	76%	60%	6%	71%
1965 qtr. 1	67%	80%	76%	60%	3%	70%
1965 qtr. 2	65%	80%	76%	57%	1%	70%
1965 qtr. 3	62%	80%	76%	56%	0%	68%

Table 4.8 presents a contrast to this, showing the value of understanding the political context for a presidential policy initiative, as well as thoroughly understanding the marginal influence of the various elements of that context. President Clinton had a Congress that was not as heavily Democratic as Johnson's. Coupled with that, he faced a more conservative public and a less impressive mandate. Further, Clinton's popularity was plummeting just as his Health Security Act was slated to come to a vote, during the third quarter of 1994. However, despite this, Table 4.8 shows that had the Clinton administration produced the health care legislation in May 1993, as it originally promised, ' victory would have been possible, using Medicare and Medicaid as a benchmark. During the second quarter of 1993, the act had a 70% increased likelihood of passage, very similar to Medicare and Medicaid in July 1965. Further,

TABLE 4.8

The Probability of the Health Security Act Passing from 1993 to 1994

Year and Quarter	Presidential Popularity	Senate Liberalism	House Liberalism	Climate	Mandate	Likelihood
1993 qtr. 1	55%	77%	62%	57%	69%	73%
1993 qtr. 2	44%	77%	62%	53%	35%	70%
1993 qtr. 3	47%	77%	62%	52%	17%	69%
1993 qtr. 4	51%	77%	62%	52%	9%	70%
1994 qtr. 1	52%	75%	61%	52%	4%	69%
1994 qtr. 2	46%	75%	61%	52%	2%	67%
1994 qtr. 3	41%	75%	61%	50%	1%	67%

recall that during this same time President Clinton successfully shepherded the North American Free Trade Agreement through Congress despite heavy opposition from liberal and conservative advocacy groups (see Jacobs and Shapiro, 2000, for a thorough discussion of this).

Immediately after Clinton's September 1993 speech introducing the Health Security Act, the increased likelihood of passage was again at 70%. However, from there, the likelihood of passage decreases so that by the time it was ready for a vote, during the third quarter of 1994, the likelihood of passage had slipped to 67%. The reason was a changing context, primarily in the mood of the public and the president's plummeting popularity. Because of these factors, coupled with the declining value of Clinton's mandate, the most ambitious health policy initiative since Medicare and Medicaid did not come to a vote. In fact, within three months of Senator George Mitchell's advice to the president to abandon the Health Security Act, the public's increasingly conservative mood was reflected in the polls, with the Democrats losing 52 seats in the House and 10 seats in the Senate (Conley, 2001; Jacobs and Shapiro, 2000).

CONCLUSION

In general, this chapter addresses a small segment of the overall system that produces the evolutionary departures from the established path dependent system of American health care policy. The broad questions addressed in this research are first whether political factors such as the attitudes of the public and elites toward health care policy affect the president's decision to propose health policy change. Second is the question of whether attitudes or adherence to a certain health policy metaphor among the public and elites coupled with attitudes of the public, toward the president, affect the success of the policy initiative. This research indicates that the president acts within and in reaction to a political context that sets the stage for policy change. In other words, the president acts as a policy entrepreneur, seizing upon conditions that allow for policy change. Further, in terms of attitudes and their impact, it is clear that political context defined as the mood of the public, the attitudes of the Congress, and the popularity of the president predicts the success of presidential initiatives to change the federal role in health policy.

Theoretically, the importance of political environment and political context is justified (Fett, 1992, 1994; Peterson, 1990). This theory is substantiated by the statistical evidence presented here, supporting the notion that contextual variables do indeed predict whether a policy is proposed, and whether a policy, once proposed, is approved. Further, a substantive analysis of the predictions using the contrasting examples of Medicare and Medicaid and the Health Security Act point to context as an important influence in the differing outcomes for these two presidential health policy initiatives. Both represented clear departures from the path dependent health policy system. Another important feature of Medicare and Medicaid, given a path dependent system, is that they had an institutional home within the Social Security Administration. Thus, although the policy change was dramatic, it actually followed an incrementalist approach. In contrast, the Health Security Act proposed the creation of new institutions and institutional arrangements. In fact, Clinton's next foray into health care, the State Childrens' Health Insurance Program, used the Medicare and Medicaid model, to create what Graig (1999) calls "the largest expansion of health insurance for children since the enactment of Medicaid in 1965" (p. 36).

Overall, this research contributes to our understanding of the president as a policy advocate along with establishing the role that attitudes of the elites and the public play in the policy-making process. While this analysis does not present a complete picture of the politics of presidential policy making, it does shed light on one segment of the process using health care as a particular policy area. Thus, the case that political context was important in the ultimate failure of the Health Security Act is established. However, like the Health Security Act itself, the reasons for its demise are more complex than this examination of the political climate reveals. Although it is possible to isolate certain elements of policy change to more easily understand the nature of the system, it is, as Lippmann (1965) suggested, a more complex process. One question that may arise is why a 71% increased likelihood of passage was enough to propel Medicare and Medicaid to passage, whereas a 67% likelihood of passage consigned the Health Security Act to defeat. The answer lies in other components of the turbulence and tumult that lead to those extraordinary times when policy advances in quanta previously unimagined.

Those other unsettled influences and actors are discussed in the succeeding chapters of this book. In chapters 5, 6, and 7, the Health Security Act, having been placed in historical context, is examined in depth. Specifically, in chapter 5, the role citizen information in policy preferences is examined, within the context of the act. In chapter 6, I take advantage of the fact that the act was the subject of a major media campaign—the "Harry and Louise" advertisements—to examine whether the presence of a clear message in opposition to the Act was able to stabilize the policy arena at the margins and prevent its passage. Finally, in chapter 7, I examine a question that I have only addressed in brief to that point, whether a media campaign, like Harry and Louise, could influence presidential vote choice. That is, could a successful media campaign and a failed policy actually influence presidential evaluations to the point that the president's reelection would be in jeopardy? With that, the study of the role of the president in policy change and the influence of the president on the policy comes full circle.

.

Chapter 5

Healthy, Wealthy, and Wise?

INTRODUCTION

The questions explored in this chapter address the failure of the Health Security Act. While the models presented in the previous chapters predict the passage of Medicare and Medicaid, they also indicate that the Health Security Act could have succeeded. However, we know that it did not. The question is Why? The answer to this question lies in a discussion that is, to quote Lippmann (1965) "too big, too complex and too fleeting for direct acquaintance" (p. 11). Nevertheless, the descriptive elements of the public unrest that ultimately propels path dependent policy systems to new plateaus can, in fact, as Lippman further observed, be reconstructed in simpler terms. The complexity of these new dimensions of understanding how policy changes is indeed intertwined with the very components of the examination of the influences on those elements that lead to change. The reconstructions of the real world presented thus far show that public opinion and political context influence policy change at the margins. The next question is whether there are additional effects on the components of public opinion and context that affect these elements at the margins. The answer to this query lies in the subtleties of public opinion where information and media exposure affect attitudes. In other words, to understand the failure of the Health Security Act, it is necessary to understand how information from various sources impacted and influenced citizens as the United States considered an evolutionary change in health care policy known as the Health Security Act.

President Clinton's campaign message of universal health care resonated with millions of citizens across the country. As the First Lady convened her health policy committee, many of those people scoured the daily papers for any news of the plan that was being molded. When the Health Security Act was finally introduced, many interested citizens ordered the *White House Summary of the Plan* and a copy of the full law. Those who read the plan, despite its complexity, were extremely excited; the Health Security Act was all that many of those Clinton voters had hoped: It was essentially crafted by public opinion and it seemed like it would provide everything that President Clinton had said it would. When the Health Security Act ultimately failed, many were perplexed. In this chapter, public support is examined as the heart of the creation and implementation of policy. However, rather than simply looking at marginal values of support for the policy change, public opinion is deconstructed into its component parts so that the unique characteristics of the population that go into the decision to support a presidential policy initiative can be examined.

Public support can make or break American public policy proposals. Although exceptions take place, elected officials generally do not stray far from what the American public supports, especially for new proposals that would alter the status quo considerably (Kingdon, 1989). For example, studies find that policy generally matches differences in state public opinion (Erickson, Wright, & McIver, 1993) and reflects changes over time in public opinion as legislators and executives shape policy to public preferences (Hartley & Russett, 1992; Page & Shapiro, 1983; Stimson, 1991; but see Jacobs & Shapiro, 2000). Other scholars show how the amount of information held by citizens affects their policy views and voting behavior (Bartels, 1996; DelliCarpini & Keeter, 1996; Lindeman, 1996). Nevertheless, there are few studies that actually link specific public knowledge of a policy to individual support for that policy, while also controlling for other factors that affect policy support (see Gilens, 2001, for a recent exploration). Further, the effects of endogenous information have not been assessed (but see Kuklinski, Metlay, & Kay, 1982).

In this chapter, theories of citizen information and support are applied by examining the most important domestic policy proposal advanced over the past two decades, the Clinton administration's health care plan: the Health Security Act (HSA). The HSA represents a clear evolutionary departure from existing health care policy in the United States. Rather than working incrementally by nesting the HSA within an existing institutional structure, the Clinton administration planned to create a new system with its own institutional components. Thus, the Health Security Act, even more so than Medicare or Medicaid, represented a clear departure from the existing health policy path in the United States and a change in the predominant metaphor that relied on a market-maximized system.

Ultimately, the HSA was defeated because it could not pass a vote in Congress, but the members of Congress were influenced greatly by changing public opinion (West, Heith, & Goodwin, 1996; but see Jacobs & Shapiro, 1994). For a few years, the public indicated in countless public opinion polls that it was ready to adopt a blend of the liberal health care as societal right and health care as an employer responsibility metaphors (Schlesinger & Lau, 2000). This is essentially what the Health Security Act promised to provide. However, as the HSA was debated, a message developed that warned that the HSA was not a blend of the two metaphors, but rather a rejection of all other metaphors in favor of health care as a societal right (Schlesinger & Lau, 2000). The role that this message played in the ultimate demise of the HSA is the focus of this chapter as well as chapters 6 and 7. Specifically, in this chapter, the focus is on the aggregate effects of individual level information (DelliCarpini & Keeter, 1996; Gilens, 2001; Jacobs & Shapiro, 2000; Schlesinger & Lau, 2000).

THEORIES OF INFORMATION

Recently, the question of what people know about politics and policy has been expanded beyond the classic Delli/Carpini and Keeter (1996) scale to discussions of domain-specific policy knowledge (see, for example, Gilens, 2001; Schlesinger & Lau, 2000), that is, moving beyond the general civics knowledge of the political world, into a system where more specific fact-based questions about public policy areas like health, education, and welfare are examined. Generally, there is the impression that measurement of political knowledge is valid and can be used as a tool to understand the political actions and preferences of citizens. There is also a movement, still somewhat embryonic, to examine whether knowledge, especially domain-specific knowledge, influences policy opinions. That is to say, are individuals who possess more knowledge about a specific policy area substantively different in their attitudes from those who possess less knowledge? (See Gilens, 2001, for an example of this research.)

While the general concept that public opinion can influence public policy is not new (Brody & Page, 1972; Carmines & Stimson, 1980; Page, 1978; Sears, Lau, Tyler, & Allen, 1980), few studies in political science link domain specific knowledge of a policy to individual support for that policy, while also controlling for other factors that affect policy support (but see Gilens, 2001; Kuklinski et al., 1982; Mutz, 1993). Most of the research on how knowledge influences political behavior has been on voting behavior and candidate evaluations. For example, some scholars examine how the amount of information held by citizens affects their policy views and voting behavior (Bartels, 1996; DelliCarpini & Keeter, 1996; Lindeman, 1996). Although Bartels (1991) notes that "the appeal of representative democracy hinges on the responsiveness of elected politicians to the preferences and interests of their constituents," there are few empirical studies examining this relationship (p. 457).

Generally, the study of how public opinion affects policy attitudes must begin with an examination of the seminal work on attitudes by Fishbein and Ajzen (1975) who offer a reinterpretation of Converse's (1964) classic investigation.

Fishbein and Ajzen not only define attitudes as negative or positive evaluations of an object, but go on to break attitudes down into identifiable, and thus quantifiable, components. (See Liska, 1984, for a critical examination of the Fishbein and Ajzen model.) Bartels (1991) finds convincing evidence for an effect of public opinion on a specific policy area at a specific point in time: defense spending during the first year of the Reagan administration. Likewise, Price and Zaller (1993) find evidence of a rise in domain-specific news recall as political sophistication increases (see also Iyengar, 1990; Zaller, 1990, 1992.)

The focus in this chapter is on the mediating effect of knowledge in a domain-specific policy area: health care. This is an especially important question, given Lau, Smith, and Fiske's (1991) findings that "the relationship between the beliefs of voters and their evaluations of policy proposals depends on the nature of the information environment" (p. 67). Specifically, like Kuklinski, Metlay, and Kay's (1982) investigation of the mediating effect of knowledge in nuclear power, I examine the role of knowledge in a similar "highly complex and highly consequential policy area" (p. 615). The authors find that knowledgeable citizens generally rely on ideology to inform their policy choices, while less knowledgeable citizens rely on general attitudes and cues from reference groups. The power of reference groups is supported by Huckfeldt and Sprague (1991), who argue that social influence among members of reference groups can impact citizen opinions (see also Grannovetter, 1973; Kenny, 1994.)

Jacoby's (1991) examination of the influence of education and political sophistication on issue attitudes supports Kuklinki, Metlay, and Kay's findings in regard to the use of ideology by more knowledgeable citizens. Jacoby writes that "ideological influence is, indeed, limited to a relatively small set of people. But for them, it has an extremely potent impact on issue attitudes and attitude consistency. What determines the presence or absence of an ideological schema? The general answer seems to be political sophistication" (p. 199). DelliCarpini and Keeter (1996) elaborate on this by examining various theories of the relationship between knowledge and political sophistication. Specifically, DelliCarpini and Keeter find "that political knowledge is a relatively unidimensional concept, that a citizen's level of factual knowledge can be gauged with a short series of survey questions" (1993, p. 1203). Overall, the authors demonstrate that political knowledge can be measured through a five-item "test" of factual knowledge.

Recent research has begun to examine not only the mediating effects of knowledge (Althaus, 1996, 1998), but also the validity of political sophistication measures (Mondak, 1999). Specifically, Althaus (1996) found that well-informed citizens could have a profound impact on policy opinion surveys when the issue population is small. In other words, when an issue is of low salience, a relatively small group of well-informed individuals can have a large impact on public opinion because the ill-informed are more likely to respond with "don't know" for low salience issues. Althaus (1998) supports this finding using National Election Study data, where he argues that political sophistication and knowledge influence marginal policy preferences at differing intensities. When a small group of citizens are highly knowledgeable, preferences are skewed toward that group more so than they would be if all citizens were well informed. Mondak (1999) confirms this by demonstrating that the coding mechanism for political sophistication, where "don't knows" are placed in the incorrect response category, may produce erroneous results.

Much of the existing literature examining knowledge or sophistication focuses on candidates rather than policies. For example, Miller, Wattenberg, and Malunchuk (1986) find that more highly educated individuals are more likely to use candidate personality criteria in the selection of a presidential candidate. The authors generally argue that through a highly complex cognitive process, knowledgeable voters use personality as an indicator of performance. Stone, Rapoport, and Atkeson (1995) add to this literature by examining how voters decide in presidential primaries when party identification is no longer an easy cue. The authors find that "voters try to reduce information costs rather than actively engaging in extensive information searches" (p. 156). They accomplish this by excluding candidates with little name recognition, initially. In terms of policy, one can imagine a similar process with less popular and less salient policies being eliminated from the choice set when there are multiple policy proposals without any clear information to be used for shortcuts in decision heuristics.

However, when there is a clear partisan message associated with a policy domain, party identification presents the possibility of an information shortcut. For example, Jacoby (1988) examines party identification as a cue in the development of attitudes. Generally, he finds that "a partisan tie provides an individual with a source for cues—perceptions of the party's issues—that are useful guidelines in the opinion formation process" (p. 657). Jacoby (1995) extends this to an examination of the ideological basis for policy attitude formation. Although he does not address the role of policy sophistication or education in his study, Jacoby firmly establishes the role of partisanship as a shortcut in attitude formation. Rahn (1993) extends this research by examining how citizens use partisan stereotypes as a simplified method to make complex political choices in elections. However, Lupia (1994) showed that low-information voters were able to mimic the actions of highly informed voters in the California insurance referendum, even in the absence of party identification, by using easily obtained cues.

Essentially, this expands the notion of the influence of reference groups (see DeSart, 1995, for example). Taking parties as a reference group, we see that strong partisans are more likely to be influenced by the messages of the reference group with which they identify, their party. However, the evidence presented by Jacoby is inconclusive in regard to whether less knowledgeable people are more likely to use partisanship to aid in attitude formation. Certainly, Lupia's finding demonstrates that alternatives to party cues exist for low-information voters. For example, McDermott (1997) shows that "in low-information races voters stereotype women candidates as more liberal than men candidates of the same party, and vote accordingly" (p. 281).

Erber and Lau (1990) find that an examination of "the ways in which people typically process political information can contribute to an explanation of changes in cynicism" (p. 250), which they define broadly as the perceived distance from a political candidate or party. Thus, the authors establish groundwork for the proposition that education, at least in terms of cognitive ability, can have an impact on how information is used in examining a reference group. Mondak (1993) expands this by examining the cognitive dynamics of policy support. Generally, he finds that in low-information policy domains, that is, domains where there is little information available to the public, citizens rely on "source cues" or policy positions favored by an elite with whom they identify. In high-information domains, the reliance on source cues diminishes dramatically. Rahn, Aldrich, and Borgida (1994) extend Mondak's findings by demonstrating that the structure and flow of information affect judgments of political candidates quite differently among low- and high-political sophistication individuals.

Gilens (2001) found that policy-specific scales are useful in understanding political behavior, writing that his analysis of general measures of sophistication leads to three conclusions:

> First, studies of political information based on general knowledge scales offer a useful but incomplete account of the effect of political ignorance. The limits of this approach arise from the fact that many people who are fully informed in terms of general political knowledge are nonetheless ignorant of policy-specific information that would alter their political judgments. Second, policy-specific ignorance may well have greater influence on political preferences than the lack of general knowledge as measured by political information scales. . . . [N]evertheless, the results suggest that much of what separates actual political preferences from hypothetical "enlightened preferences" is due to ignorance of specific policy-relevant facts, not a lack of general political knowledge or the cognitive skills or orientations that measures of general political information reflect. Third, policy-specific information has a stronger influence on respondents who display higher levels of general political knowledge. Rather than dilute the effect of new information, general knowledge (and the cognitive capacities it reflects) appears to facilitate its incorporation into political judgments. (p. 380)

Overall, Gilens presents an argument for the use of domain-specific policy-sophistication measures as indicators of policy preferences, while noting that these measures, like general political sophistication scales, reflect the cognitive ability of citizens. Thus, any use of domain-specific sophistication measures must also take into account the ability to obtain and process information.

There are numerous notions about how information affects attitudes and numerous theories about how information is obtained. Generally speaking, the literature explains how highly sophisticated individuals became knowledgeable and how low-sophistication individuals use various cues to mimic the behavior of well-informed individuals. However, there are few explanations of whether or how information changes policy attitudes (see Gilens, 2001).

THE FAILURE OF THE HEALTH SECURITY ACT

The 1992 presidential election brought the issue of health care to the forefront of the American political agenda, especially after Senator Harris Wofford of Pennsylvania won a special election that focused on the development of a national health care program. Skocpol (1993) termed this the "focusing event" (see Kingdon, 1984) for health care reform (see also Brown, 1994, p. 198). At that time, the Health Care Financing Administration reported that medical costs consumed 14% of American Gross National Product, with continued increases predicted, despite the fact that nearly 40 million Americans had no health insurance. The media covered these issues extensively, making health care policy highly salient.

President Clinton appointed First Lady Hillary Clinton to lead a task force to develop health care legislation that would ensure universal access at low cost while maintaining quality. The long and visible development process included hundreds of advisers, and, in late September 1993, President Clinton presented the HSA to Congress in a televised speech. Afterward, Clinton promoted the HSA, which was published and summarized widely, across the United States, answering questions in the kind of town hall meetings in which he excelled as a persuasive communicator. Though its 1,400 pages were numbing in their detail, Americans had access to more information about the HSA than perhaps any other public program proposal.

Initially, the Republican response was muted. This was, in part, as Jacobs and Shapiro (2000) explain, a strategy designed "to balance their electoral and policy goals: their commitment to protecting the party's reputation among centrist voters and the party's prospects in upcoming elections clashed with the objective of conservatives to block all health reform" (p. 131). Thus, as time passed, the Republicans tried to mold the opinions of centrist voters so that Republican opposition to health care reform would not harm electoral chances in 1994. Jacobs and Shapiro describe this as a "dual strategy of both responding to and shaping public opinion" (p. 131).

Ultimately, two sets of opponents fought the HSA. First, Republican leadership in the Congress and conservative political commentators lambasted it, both delivering messages about restricted choice and forced participation in government-sponsored cooperative buying plans. The second group, led by the health care and health insurance industry, echoed these messages in an effective national advertising campaign that started even before Clinton's speech, soon dubbed as "Harry and Louise." (For experimental studies showing the effectiveness of simple negative health care advertisements, see Cobb & Kuklinski, 1997.) Pressure by these groups had defeated previous attempts to move toward national health insurance (see, Kelley, 1956, for example).

In the end, the HSA was not brought up for a vote in Congress and it became viewed as the biggest failure of the Clinton administration. Scholars offer several explanations for its failure. Hanson et al.'s (1996) survey of congressional members and staffs found that 20% thought the HSA was "too big, too sweeping, too much government control," another 13% said it was "too complex, public didn't understand," while 13% attributed the failure to interest group lobbying and advertising (pp. 140–141). This study also reports that the factors which were reported to have the greatest influence on the debate were, in order, the Clinton administration at 80%, public opinion at 75%, advertising by interest groups at 55%, and political parties at 47% (p. 142). Brodie (1996) attributes the failure of the HSA to a lack of participation by congressional groups who should have actively supported the plan, such as liberals (14% participation) and Democrats (20% participation). Participation by these groups should have effectively countered HSA opponents, conservatives (20%) and Republicans (20%).

Congress was influenced strongly by public opinion. West et al. (1996) examined the media effects, finding that countervalent ads moved public opinion from 79% in favor in April 1993, during the task force process, to 59% favorable in September to 52% favorable in October. Jacobs and Shapiro (1994) show public opinion declining considerably in October, before returning to earlier levels, arguing that "the fluctuations may reflect Americans' genuine confusion about the Clinton plan; large majorities of respondents (70–85%) repeatedly acknowledge that they understand little or nothing about it" (p. 211).

While Congress might have passed this legislation despite the decline of favorable public opinion, such action is unlikely for sweeping legislation. Generally, Kingdon (1989) argues that public opinion influences Congress as "congressmen rely most heavily on *colleagues* [italics added] within the House and on *constituents* [italics added] for guidance as they vote, other actors in the system such as lobbyists and administration policy makers tend to work through these two gatekeeper sources" (p. 240). Peterson (1994) argued that the Clinton administration failed to fully understand the structure of Congress (pp. 203–204), leading to an agenda-setting problem (see also Hacker, 1997, pp. 170–173). Brady and Buckley (1995) argued that the Clinton plan was simply "too liberal" to persuade the median voter in the Senate.

These arguments suggest that one important reason for the failure of the HSA was the inability to persuade public opinion (i.e., the public) to deliver a clear message to Congress in favor of the proposal. Most explanations of the failure of the HSA point to the information that was presented by both sides as important, and the complexity of the plan. The HSA debate clearly illustrates Zaller's (1992) two-sided information flows (pp. 186–187). Although the time frame was shorter than his Vietnam War example, the HSA followed Zaller's model of ebb and flow of support based on the dissemination of information by supporters and opponents. Liberal opinion leaders advanced health care reform, and conservative opinion leaders initially joined in support for some reform, as demonstrated by the plethora of Republican health care bills introduced in Congress. President Clinton intensified the message and raised the stakes by committing publicly to development of a plan. After the plan was introduced, the countervalent message was defined by the conservative opinion and health care industry leaders, resulting in issue polarization, in which the debate was driven to two extremes represented by ideological labels (Zaller, 1992, p. 186). Information and misinformation presented in the countervalent message may have led to the ultimate defeat of the HSA. I test this notion by examining the role of accurate information in promoting support for the plan.

INFORMATION AND POLICY SUPPORT

Using the HSA as an empirical example that focused on the role of the president, the parties, and media information campaigns, three basic theories of information and policy support are jointly tested. First, the role of cuing by examining party identification is considered. Second, the role of elite signaling (the receptivity to which I measure by presidential vote preference in 1992) is explored. Finally, the role of actual knowledge of the HSA is examined.

Cuing theory describes what is perhaps the easiest way for the uninformed to make informed choices. A simple cue would be seeking out others like oneself and following their lead (Granovetter, 1985; Kuklinski & Hurley, 1994; Petty & Caciopo, 1986; Popkin, 1991; Zaller, 1987). An example of cuing theory is the use of partisanship as a determinant of which policy positions to support. Lupia (1994) illustrated how voters made choices on a California insurance referendum by using cues from different groups instead of expending financial and cognitive resources to obtain firsthand information. However, Kuklinski et al. (1982) find that such cues can be subject to misinterpretation and are not perfect substitutes for full information. In my study, if simple cuing is important, respondents identifying themselves as Democrats should show more support for the HSA.

Second, and related to cues, political leaders rely on citizen faith that their signals will comport with simple perceptions of reality, such as whether their situation or that of the nation will improve or decline under a new policy. Zaller

(1987) argues that acceptance of elite messages is dependent on exposure and source (p. 824), although Kuklinski and Hurley (1994) use experiments to show that signals from identifiable political leaders can, at times, lead to errors in decisions. Those who supported Clinton for president in 1992 (controlling for party identification) should show more support for his HSA.

The third theory focuses on our main area of interest, actual policy knowledge. Those who know more about a policy may be likely to support it more or less. Political scientists have long emphasized how little the average citizen knows about politics and policy (e.g., Berelson, Lazarsfeld, & McPhee, 1954; Lazarsfeld, Berelson, & Gaudet, 1954). Moving beyond aggregate knowledge, however, Zaller (1992) notes that a more careful analysis of the literature shows that some number of citizens are generally well informed while another group is woefully uninformed, with the largest group of citizens somewhere in the middle (Bennett, 1989; Converse, 1990; DelliCarpini & Keeter, 1996; Smith, 1989). Those with more education and higher incomes tend to be more informed about political issues (DelliCarpini & Keeter, 1996). However, knowledge of political candidates and institutions that most studies test may be less important to citizens than specific policies of government that affect them. Kuklinski et al. (1996) note that "surprisingly . . . researchers have not focused heavily on factual knowledge about policies . . . choosing instead to collect data on people's text-book knowledge about institutions . . . and processes" (p. 2). In one of the few such studies, for a highly salient (after Three Mile Island), but complex, nuclear power issue, Kuklinski et al. (1982) found that few citizens were well informed about basic issues, but those who were informed supported different policies than those less well informed.

For our purposes, what is important is how actual knowledge of the policy influences support for it. The complex HSA attempted to address several health care problems at the same time, using elements of both market and government provision. One would expect those who possess more actual knowledge about the HSA will generally show different levels of support for the plan than those with less actual knowledge. But it is also true that supporters may also be more likely to learn more about the plan. Thus, a reciprocal relationship between knowledge and support might exist: Those who know more about the HSA may also be more likely to support it, while those who support the HSA may be more likely to seek information and thus be more knowledgeable about it. This relationship is explored in the next section.

MEASURING AND TESTING KNOWLEDGE

How to measure citizen knowledge is not obvious. DelliCarpini and Keeter (1996) and Zaller (1986) argue that political knowledge can be measured by a domain-specific five-item scale. This general technique is applied to knowledge about the HSA.

The data come from *The Washington Post* Health Care Poll of October 1993,[1] a national poll of households in the contiguous United States conducted soon after the introduction of Clinton's HSA. The target population consisted of all adults over the age of 18. There were 1,015 total respondents. For some questions, most notably 1992 vote choice, the sample was split with every other person contacted answering alternating sets of questions. All respondents were asked the basic demographic and opinion questions. As Table 5.1 shows, with vote choice the data matched the actual election results well with 43% saying they supported Bill Clinton, 33% saying they supported George Bush, and 17% saying they supported Ross Perot.[2]

Respondents were asked five questions on various aspects of the HSA to determine their knowledge.[3] Responses to these questions are shown in simple frequencies and bivariate relationships in Table 5.1 and Table 5.2. Some 168 of the respondents (about 25%) answered one question correctly, while only three (0.4%) of the respondents answered all five questions about the HSA correctly (see Table 5.1).

Table 5.2 illustrates the simple bivariate relationship of support and the information models. Related to cuing, the HSA received its highest level of partisan support among Democrats (51.4%), and in terms of elite signals, 64.7% of Clinton voters supported it. The knowledge variable shows that support increases for each correct response up to four correct responses, where support reaches its peak.

An interesting feature of Table 5.2 is the examination of support along party lines versus support in terms of elite influence—for example, the comparison between Democrats (51.4%) who supported the HSA and Clinton voters (64.7%) who supported the HSA. This sets the stage for failure, given the importance of party coherence in the passage of a major policy change. Of the core group of expected supporters, only a little more than half supported the plan. This was in part because other Democratic elites had plans of their own, ranging from Paul Wellstone's single-payer plan to James Cooper's managed-competition plan. Thus, Democratic elites delivered a muddled message.

A MODEL OF RECIPROCAL CAUSATION

To obtain knowledge, one must be exposed to a source of information. This basic notion can be extended to the policy arena by examining acceptance of a message as partly a function of knowledge. This suggests some motivated reasoning (Kunda, 1990) in which people are inspired to learn about areas that

TABLE 5.1
Frequencies of the Variables ($N = 680$)

Variable	Number of Observations	Percent
Support	354	52.1
Party ID		
Democrat	252	37.1
Republican	203	29.9
Independent	225	33.1
President 1992		
Clinton	292	42.9
Bush	226	33.2
Perot	117	17.2
Knowledge		
Correct Responses:		
None	93	13.7
One	168	24.7
Two	213	31.3
Three	137	20.2
Four	66	9.7
Five	3	0.4
Education		
High School or less	277	40.7
Some college	330	48.5
Graduate or professional	73	10.7
Income		
Poor	63	9.3
Lower middle class	199	29.3
Upper middle class	338	49.7
Wealthy	80	11.8

fit their agenda. Such a system also suggests reciprocal causality between support for a policy and knowledge about that policy.

Knowledge, of course, is not free. Rather, to gain knowledge one must expend resources, including money, or simply cognitive effort, all of which are limited. One would expect education and income to influence support for the HSA, as they provide powerful constraints on the information a citizen can obtain and process. They also affect support through knowledge in a nonrecursive manner. Further, the interactions that one might expect between the variables are captured in the model itself.

Figure 5.1 implies a nonrecursive system of equations, in which two variables exhibit reciprocal causation.[4] The following nonrecursive system of equations is

TABLE 5.2
Support for the HSA by Cuing and Signaling Factors
and Actual Knowledge

	Support for Health Security Act	
	Percent	N
Cuing Factors		
Democrat	51.4	182
Republican	16.4	58
Independent	32.2	114
President 1992		
Clinton	64.7	229
Bush	13.3	47
Perot	22.0	78
Knowledge Correct Responses		
None	8.8	31
One	30.0	75
Two	59.1	103
Three	83.7	87
Four	99.4	56
Five	100.0	2

Note: Percentages for the cuing factors are row and percentages for knowledge are cumulative

designed to purge the estimates of the variables exhibiting reciprocal causation (*Knowledge* and *Support*) of their correlations with the error term of the equation in which they are the dependent variables:

$$\text{Knowledge} = \beta_{10} + \beta_{11} \text{ Support} + \gamma_{11} \text{ Income} + \gamma_{12} \text{ Education} + \mu_1 \quad (5.1)$$

$$\text{Support} = \beta_{20} + \beta_{22} \text{ Knowledge} + \gamma_{23} \text{ Democrat} + \gamma_{24} \text{ Republican} + \gamma_{25} \text{ Clinton} + \gamma_{26} \text{ Bush} + \mu_2 \quad (5.2)$$

The overall model is estimated using the Two-Stage-Conditional-Maximum-Likelihood (2SCML) technique developed by Rivers and Vuong

FIGURE 5.1
The Nonrecursive Model

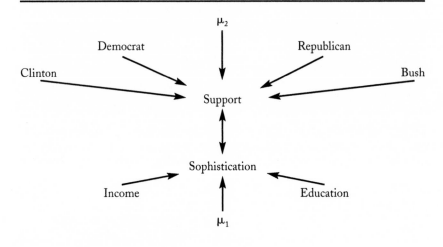

TABLE 5.3
Two-Stage-Conditional-Maximum-Likelihood
(Support as Dependent Variable) ($N = 680$)

	β	SE
Information		
Knowledge	1.204***	.252
Cuing		
Democrat	.275	.149
Republican	.018	.162
Clinton	.729***	.149
Bush	−.695***	.159
Residuals	.130	.945
Constant	.683***	.204
Log Likelihood = −333.434		
Percent Correctly Predicted = 73.33		
Reduction in Error = 48.1		

***$p < .001$.

(1988) and refined by Alvarez (1994). It is an improvement over two-stage-least-squares estimations for situations that involve estimation of a dichotomous dependent variable, when linear probability and probit models have problems.

RESULTS

Table 5.3 presents the 2SCML results. Most of the findings confirm the hypotheses. Knowledge has a substantial and nonlinear effect. Holding all other variables at their minimum, the effect on the average probability of support for the HSA of moving from zero to five correct answers on the Knowledge scale is 45%. The effect is greater moving from the modal category of two correct answers to five correct answers than for moving from answering no questions correctly to answering two correctly (27% versus 18%). The effect of having more knowledge is about the same for Clinton voters as for Bush voters (38% versus 35%). Confirming the elite signaling model, a Clinton vote increases the probability of supporting the HSA by 27%, while a Bush vote decreases the probability by 17% on average, holding all other variables at zero.[5]

Perhaps the most interesting finding is the overall effect of actual knowledge on support, given additional cues and signals. One would expect that a Republican who voted for Bush in 1992 would provide the lowest level of support for the HSA. This is true: as Table 5.4 illustrates, a Republican Bush voter has an average probability of supporting the HSA of 9%, holding all other variables at their minimum. However, increasing Knowledge from zero to the modal category more than doubles the probability of support (19%), while full Knowledge has a fivefold effect with the probability of support increasing to

TABLE 5.4

Predicted Probabilities Comparing Single-Equation Probit Results and Two-Stage-Conditional-Maximum-Likelihood (Support as Dependent Variable)

Democrat Party Identification	Republican Party Identification	Clinton Voter	Bush Voter	Knowledge	Single Probit	2SCML
Yes	No	Yes	No	0 correct	.641	.626
Yes	No	Yes	No	2 correct	.800	.788
Yes	No	Yes	No	5 correct	.941	.933
No	Yes	No	Yes	0 correct	.092	.087
No	Yes	No	Yes	2 correct	.198	.192
No	Yes	No	Yes	5 correct	.444	.440

44% on average, holding all other variables at their minimum. Table 5.4 also shows that, while the 2SCML model is the correct one, the predicted support results are fairly similar to those for a simple one-stage probit model that does not address the issue of reciprocal causation.[6] However, it should be noted that the elaborate methodology is not introducing a finding that is not present in a simple one-stage model. Instead, the value of using 2SCML is that it refines a relationship that already exists, granting us greater confidence in our parameter estimates. Thus, one can state with more certainty that actual knowledge of the policy itself increases the probability of support substantially for all individuals, even those with the greatest disposition to oppose the HSA, absent any knowledge.

CONCLUSION

In addition to building on the few studies of information and policy support by modeling HSA knowledge and support as endogenous in a reciprocal relationship, with income and education serving as instruments for knowledge, this model presents a clear and plausible story of how public opinion mediated by misinformation led to the demise of the Clinton health care plan. Citizens with greater education and income were better informed and, according to other studies, better able to process information (DelliCarpini & Keeter, 1996; Gilens, 2001; Zaller, 1992). Here, the results indicate that accurate knowledge, "purified" of the contaminating effects of education and income, still has a large impact on policy support for all categories of voters. Clinton was able to inform some voters about the HSA and they were much more likely to support it. Something that was even true for Republicans who did not vote for Clinton. These results are supported by Gilens (2001) who writes that his findings "do not contradict the belief that elite cues are more important in shaping the public's political judgments than are raw policy-relevant facts. But they do suggest that, at least for the more politically knowledgeable and sophisticated segments of the public, the influence of raw facts can be substantial" (p. 392).

Countervalent advertisements sponsored by HSA opponents, however, appear to have confused many voters' information about the HSA, which then reduced their support (see chapter 5). Americans do not decide national policy by referendum. Ultimately, Congress did not feel that it had enough public support to pass legislation that represented such a major change from the status quo.

This finding suggests that voter information campaigns can be extremely important to generating support for policies. The presidential "bully pulpit" is no more than a vague idea but can be used actively to generate policy support among the public. While political scientists and other analysts view Clinton as a very effective communicator, the HSA may have been too complex for even him to explain adequately to a sufficient number of citizens for them to understand well enough to withstand strong attacks from opponents (see Cobb & Kuklinski, 1997). Clinton has reflected that one of his two largest first-term mistakes was "poor presentation" of the HSA and failure to anticipate the strength of opposition to it (see Bennet, 1997). Opponents of the HSA were able to provide their own countervalent information against it, to confuse enough voters to make public support decline.

Overall, the results in this chapter explore whether the top down versus bottom up debate about support for public policy should instead focus on the origins and use of information. By integrating existing theories of information use and showing that they are applicable to the realm of policy support, it is possible to gain greater insight into why and how policy proposals that are designed to tap into public unrest and thereby propel policy from an existing equilibrium along a path dependent route can fail because of information. Finally, the results confirm existing studies on information in that it is clear that in the absence of firsthand information, people use defaults available in information processing to make decisions regarding public policy, relying on various shortcuts. However, the two stage model indicates that while education and income effects are not significant in terms of actual support for a given policy, these factors work through Knowledge to influence support.

These findings support Simon (1995) and North (1990) and others who have refined information theories by examining the limits that cognitive and economic endowments place on choice. Those who can buy or process more information do so. These people then become greatly informed about a public policy, using their knowledge to make decisions about public policy. Others without the resources rely those with knowledge and political elites to make their own informed choices.

In the remaining chapters, information is again used as a general context for the examination of how policy changes in a path dependent system. In the analyses that follow, having made our way through various levels of complexity in an attempt to discover the components of the turbulence that ultimately has the power to propel policy along a new evolutionary path, the focus turns to media effects. The studies presented in chapters 6 and 7 rely on two methods of data: The first study in each chapter uses survey data, which has higher external validity, and the second study uses data collected in an experiment with higher internal validity. Overall, the two types of data are used to explore media effects and media priming. Iyengar and Kinder (1987) define media priming as "changes in the standards that people use to make political evaluations" (p. 63) as a result of exposure to media coverage, which indeed is the missing component of the examination presented thus far.

Chapter 6

Examining the Impact of Countervalent Messages on Policy Support

How "Harry and Louise" Changed Public Opinion

INTRODUCTION

In the previous chapter, the notion that domain-specific political sophistication (see Gilens, 2001) mediates public opinion of the Health Security Act
was explored within the context of instances of dynamic policy change wherein
health care policy departs from the path dependent system settling on some new
plateau (Baumgartner & Jones, 1993; North, 1990; Schneider & Teske, 1995).
In that setting, information was treated as one of the components of the underlying turbulence that North (1990) describes as the pool from which potential
policy change emerges. The conclusion was that information about the Health
Security Act did indeed play a significant role in its ultimate failure. In this
chapter, the role of information, or more accurately, misinformation, is examined
more closely. Generally, the model presented in the previous chapter indicates
that knowledge, gained from various sources, mediates policy opinions. That is,
levels of knowledge influence policy opinions in differing ways, with factual or
seemingly factual information being the most important predictor of ultimate
support for a policy. In this chapter, the role of incorrect information, presented
as fact and the subsequent impact on policy support is examined. Without giving away the story, it should be noted that the finding presented in this chapter,
is consistent with Ansolabehere et al.'s (1994) finding, albeit in a slightly different context, that attack advertising demobilizes the electorate and deflates candidate support by approximately 5%. Further, a return to the notion of policy

sophistication as a dominant force, even in the presence of media messages, is explored within an experimental setting in the second part of this chapter. Again, the findings are consistent with existing literature (Aldrich, Sullivan, & Borgida, 1989; Ansolabehere & Iyengar, 1994; Ansolabehere et al., 1994; Chard & Ling, 1999; Iyengar & Kinder, 1987; Jacobs & Shapiro, 1994, 2000; Krosnick & Kinder, 1990; McGraw & Ling, 2002; Neuman, Just, & Crigler, 1992). In a nutshell, the results in this chapter demonstrate the effects of media coverage in shaping and molding public opinion—that is, under what conditions do effects occur and how do they relate to policy change in the United States health care policy system.

MEDIA EFFECTS: NEGATIVE ADVERTISING AND "HARRY AND LOUISE"

To this point, the role of public support in making and breaking policy proposals has been established. While there is obviously the potential for the types of evolutionary policy change that North (1990) discusses, as noted earlier, elected officials generally do not stray far from what the American public supports, especially when facing new proposals that would alter the status quo considerably (Kingdon, 1989). Thus, as the studies presented in chapters 3, 4, and 5 show, although there are times when policy can and does change rapidly, those occurrences are rare and they are predicated on the notion that there will be a sufficient degree of tumult in the foundation of the existing policy system to support a dramatic change in policy. The previous chapters took various components of the foundation apart to examine what factors may contribute to such turbulence that policy had to change, or in contrast, what elements of the foundation could be rattled until the opportunity for change arose. Consistently throughout these examinations, public opinion has been presented as a mediating force, that is, a force that can affect policy change at the margins.

The notion that public opinion is important to policy change is supported in the literature. For example, Erickson, Wright, and McIver (1993) find that public policy generally matches the preferences exhibited in state-level public opinion. Likewise, Stimson (1999), Hartley and Russett (1992), and Page and Shapiro (1983) show that policy reflects changes over time in public opinion as legislators and executives shape policy to public preferences. Other scholars have added information as a key component of this process. Specifically, Bartels (1996) and others (DelliCarpini & Keeter, 1996; Gilens, 2001; Lindeman, 1996) show how the amount of information held by citizens affects their policy views and voting behavior. Jacobs and Shapiro (2000) have added the innovative concept of "crafted talk," which is the authors' term for attempts to mold public opinion by politicians and interest groups.

Crafted talk is necessarily intertwined with the idea of media priming (see generally Iyengar & Kinder, 1987). However, as Jacobs and Shapiro (2000) explain, it is much more sophisticated than that, and is used by politicians and interest groups alike. Writing specifically about the Harry and Louise campaign, the authors state:

> A particularly memorable illustration of interest groups' use of crafted presentations to pressure politicians was the "Harry and Louise" health care advertisement, which portrayed a fictional couple worrying over the impact of the Clinton health plan. The Health Insurance Association of America (HIAA) sponsored the spots because, one of its vice presidents explained [that it] "allowed a little old trade association to have an impact way beyond its size." (p. 47)

Jacobs and Shapiro go on to explain that "interest groups, legislators, and others use political advertisements to stir up public attention and support for their policy goals" (p. 47). This summation is really at the heart of the notion of how policy changes in a path dependent system. As I have argued in previous chapters, the tumult and turbulence that North (1990) describes as a necessary predecessor to evolutionary policy change has its origins in "stirring up" public opinion. One way that this can be accomplished is through the media and to that end, the investigations presented in this chapter (and the next) rest in media priming.

Simply stated, media priming is the psychological process whereby people formulate and revise their opinions as a result of exposure to the juxtaposition of issues in the media (Iyengar, 1991; McGraw & Ling, 2001). That is, the more prominent an issue is in the media, the greater the weight it will be given in making political judgments (Iyengar, 1991). Specifically, priming refers to the impact of news coverage on the weight assigned to specific issues in making political judgments (Iyengar, 1991, 133). There are a number of studies conducted both in the laboratory and in the real world that demonstrate the existence of priming (Iyengar & Kinder, 1987; Iyengar et al., 1984; Krosnick & Kinder, 1990).

Within these studies, the most firmly established effects are based on evidence that people evaluate the president differently after exposure to coverage that emphasizes different policy issues like defense, energy, and the economy, or scandals such as the Iran Contra Affair. Generally, media attention to an issue increases the accessibility of the issue in recipients' minds and consequently leads them to consider the issue in their evaluations of the president.

The accepted explanation is that priming is based solely on people's use of the accessibility heuristic in making political judgments. Essentially, people use whatever issue is most salient to form evaluations (Fischoff, Slovic, & Lichtenstein, 1980; Higgins & King, 1981). The implication of this is that frequent media attention to an issue causes the person to change their standards of evaluation to include the issue as a criterion. For example, exposure to media coverage about health care will lead people to use health care as an issue by which to evaluate the president in the following years in addition to or instead of some other issue.

Much of the priming literature focuses on evaluations of the president, or in some remote cases, other politicians; however, few studies examine the effect of the media on policy approval. (For a full discussion of priming and the president, please refer to chapter 7.) These studies provide clear evidence for issue priming; however, they raise a very important, yet unanswered, question of the potential applications of priming. In other words, the robustness of priming has not been demonstrated beyond evaluations of the president. More explicitly, little research has been done showing the effects of priming on political behavior. However, Ansolabehere et al. (1994) have found effects from negative campaign advertisements on intentions to vote. Generally, the authors argue that "campaigns can be either mobilizing or demobilizing events, *depending on the nature of the messages they generate*" (p. 829). Ansolabehere et al. test this using an experimental design in which they change the tone of the message from negative to positive. Overall, they find that negative advertising deflates intention to vote for any candidate by a consistent 5%. Thus, it is possible that negative advertising campaigns, like the Harry and Louise ads, can influence political behavior. Ansolabehere et al. demonstrate this effect only in the context of a political campaign between two candidates, not in a campaign over a policy. Nevertheless, Jacobs and Shapiro (2000) show that politicians and interest groups believe that there may indeed be an influence on policy:

> A priming approach concentrates on raising the priority and the weight that individuals assign to particular attitudes already stored in their memories. Politicians use public statements and the press coverage they can generate to influence which attitudes and information individuals retrieve from memory and incorporate into their judgments. For instance, opponents of health reform consistently voiced the warning that the Clinton plan would create "big government," intending to prompt many Americans to put whatever conservative attitudes they harbored toward government to the forefront of their minds and to use them as the yardstick by which to evaluate health reform. The political fight, then was over the salience of different yardsticks that the public would use in its evaluation. (p. 50)

In the case of the Clinton plan, the yardstick can be likened to the health policy metaphors (Schlesinger & Lau, 2000) discussed in previous chapters. That is, on one hand, there is the "status quo/market maximized" yardstick versus Clinton's "health care as a societal right" yardstick. The general goal of this research is to explain how media coverage of health care influences public opinion, which in turn affected whether health care reform would occur in the United States.

THE MEDIA AND THE HEALTH SECURITY ACT

The 1992 presidential election brought the issue of health care to the fore-front of the American political agenda, especially after Senator Harris Wofford of Pennsylvania won a special election that focused on the development of a national health care program. Skocpol (1993) termed this the "focusing event" (see also Kingdon, 1984) generally for health care reform (see also Brown, 1994, p. 198). At that time, the Health Care Financing Administration reported that medical costs consumed 14% of American gross national product, with continued increases predicted, despite the fact that nearly 40 million Americans had no health insurance. The media covered these issues extensively, making health care policy highly salient.

In another news-grabbing turn of events, President Clinton appointed First Lady Hillary Clinton to lead a task force to develop health care legislation that aimed to ensure universal access at low cost while maintaining quality. Of course, the use of the first lady in such a political role captured nearly as much attention as the issue of health care reform itself. The long and visible development process included hundreds of advisers, and, in late September 1993, President Clinton presented the HSA to Congress in a televised speech. In fact, Jacobs and Shapiro (2000) discuss this speech at length as an example of a "crafted presentation" designed as a media prime (p. 47). Following his speech, Clinton promoted the Health Security Act widely, although with less zeal than his aides had hoped (Jacobs & Shapiro, 2000). As I discussed in previous chapters, two sets of opponents fought the HSA. First, Republican leadership in the Congress and conservative political commentators lambasted it, both delivering messages about restricted choice and forced participation in government-sponsored cooperative buying plans, thereby priming the yardstick by which the public measured health care policy proposals. The second group, led by the health care and health insurance industries, echoed these messages in an effective national advertising campaign that started even before Clinton's speech, soon dubbed as "Harry and Louise" (for experimental studies showing the effectiveness of simple negative health care advertisements, see Cobb & Kuklinski, 1997). These opponents and their rapid rise are predicted by Jacobs and Shapiro's (2000) crafted talk model. In fact, the authors write that such a response to Clinton's September 1993 speech was inevitable (p. 47). The Harry and Louise advertisements were themselves an example of crafted talk as Jacobs and Shapiro explain: "HIAA hired public opinion analysts to maximize the impact of their 'Harry and Louise' ads on Americans and to pinpoint the most appealing presentation, investigating whether the couple should sit in a community center, a living room, or a kitchen" (p. 49). In the end, the Harry and Louise ads depicted an average American couple who discussed health care policy. The advertisements featured issues such as choice of doctor, access to specialists, and costs.

Given the crafted nature of the campaign, it should come as no surprise that all of these issues resonated with the public, and according to West, Heath, and Goodwin (1996), they had the desired negative effect. Ultimately, the HSA was not brought up for a vote in Congress and it became viewed as the biggest failure of the Clinton administration. Scholars offer several explanations for its failure. Hanson et al.'s (1996) survey of congressional members and their staffs found that 20% thought the HSA was "too big, too sweeping, too much government control," another 13% said it was "too complex, public didn't understand," while 13% attributed the failure to interest group lobbying and advertising (pp. 140–141). This study also found that the factors that were reported to have the greatest influence on the debate were, in order, the Clinton administration at 80%, public opinion at 75%, advertising by interest groups at 55%, and political parties at 47% (p. 142). Finally, the Harry and Louise advertisements and their priming of a new yardstick, by which the public measures health policy initiatives, were sufficient to drive away politicians who had been only tacit supporters (Jacobs & Shapiro, 2000).

Congress was influenced strongly by public opinion (Brodie, 1996; West et al., 1996). West et al. (1996) examined the media effects, finding that countervalent ads moved public opinion from 79% in favor in April 1993 (during the task force process) to 59% favorable in September to 52% favorable in October. By February 1994, the time when the Harry and Louise advertisements were broadcast most frequently, Gallup (1994) polls showed public opinion moving against the HSA, and by July 1994 only 40% favored it, with 56% opposed. Jacobs and Shapiro (1994) argue that "the fluctuations may reflect Americans' genuine confusion about the Clinton plan; large majorities of respondents (70–85%) repeatedly acknowledge that they understand little or nothing about it" (p. 211). This created an ideal environment for priming to have an impact. By August 1994, the official start of the 1994 congressional campaign, Senator George Mitchell informed the White House that the HSA did not have the votes to pass in the Senate.

The Harry and Louise advertisements were broadcast during the critical opinion formation period for the Health Security Act, in the four months following the official introduction of the bill. According to West et al. (1996), the misinformation in the advertisements went unchallenged in the media (pp. 49–50). In fact, as Jacobs and Shapiro (2000) report, "part of HIAA's success stemmed from parlaying its paid 'Harry and Louise' ads into much greater 'free' media coverage of the ads themselves" (p. 123). I ask whether this adver-tisement, coupled with the media attention it received, had the power to derail the Health Security Act. I find that it did. (For evidence contrary to this finding, albeit in the context of an experimental political campaign, see Ansolabehere & Iyengar, 1994).

STUDY ONE: TESTING THE STRENGTH OF THE COUNTERVALENT INFORMATION MESSAGE

In the previous chapter, the notion that the role of actual fact-based knowledge of the HSA, coming from Clinton's valent message, had some power to create support for the plan was explored. In this chapter, the question of whether the information in the countervalent message from the Harry and Louise advertisements had an effect on citizen policy support is investigated (see also Jacobs & Shapiro, 2000).

To examine this question, I analyze data from a February 1994 *Washington Post* poll. This is a national poll of households in the contiguous United States conducted soon after the introduction of Clinton's HSA. The target population consisted of all adults over the age of 18.[1] Of the 511 respondents, 210 (about 41%) reported having seen the Harry and Louise advertisement and thus were exposed directly to the countervalent message, purified of any elite or party identification effects that may cloud the reception.

While overall support for the Clinton plan was about 37%, mirroring the drop in support among the general public by this time (see Table 6.1), the HSA continued to draw its greatest support from Democrats (60%) and Clinton vot-ers (73%). Most interesting is the disparity in support for the HSA between those exposed to the Harry and Louise ad and those not exposed. While both categories show less than majority levels of support, opponents outnumber supporters by two to one among those exposed to the message compared with the three to two ratio among those not exposed. Thus, it seems that there is in-dication of a priming effect exhibited at the marginals.

To examine this potential effect, I modeled this relationship in a manner parallel to the previous analysis, using the following equation:[2]

$$\text{Support} = \beta_0 + \beta_1 \text{ Ad Exposure} + \beta_3 \text{ Democrat} + \beta_4 \text{ Republican} + \\ \beta_5 \text{ Clinton} + \beta_6 \text{ Dole} + \beta_7 \text{ Income} + \beta_8 \text{ Education} + \mu_5 \quad (6.1)$$

Table 6.2 shows the results from this 1994 data. As expected, Ad Exposure is significant and negative, indicating that exposure to the countervalent mes-sage, in the form of the Harry and Louise media ad, had the power to diminish support for the HSA.

TABLE 6.1

Support for the Health Security Act by Party Identification,
1996 Vote Intention and Exposure to Harry and Louise ($N = 511$)

	Support for Health Security Act	
	Percent	N
Party Identification		
Democrat	60.3	94
Republican	15.7	24
Independent	36.1	73
President 1996		
Clinton	72.6	146
Dole	9.4	18
Counter-valent Message		
Exposed	33.3	70
Not Exposed	40.2	121

Note: Percentages are row.

TABLE 6.2

Single Stage Probit Estimation of Equation Three (Support for
the Health Security Act as Dependent Variable) ($N = 511$)

	β	SE
Information		
Adexposure	−0.299**	.137
Party Identification		
Democrat	.111	.161
Republican	−.084	.185
Clinton	1.289***	.171
Dole	−.580***	.189
Income	−.002	.003
Education	.084	.061
Constant	.778***	.240
Log Likelihood = −237.060		
Percent Correctly Predicted = 76.4		
Reduction in Error = 51.5		

$**p < .05$; $***p < .001$

TABLE 6.3
Predicted Probabilities of Support for the Health Security Act Comparing Exposure
to Countervalent Message Group with Nonexposure Group

Democrat Party Identification	Republican Party Identification	Clinton Voter	Dole Voter	Ad Exposure	Single Probit
Yes	No	Yes	No	Yes	.961
Yes	No	Yes	No	No	.912
No	Yes	No	Yes	Yes	.420
No	Yes	No	Yes	No	.371

Table 6.3 further demonstrates this impact. Taking two extremes, a Clinton Democrat and a Dole Republican, we see that exposure to the purified countervalent message decreased support for the HSA by about 5% in both cases (see Ansolabehere et al., 1994). For example, a Clinton Democrat had a 96% probability of supporting the HSA when not exposed to the ad, holding all other variables constant. This decreased to an average probability of support of 91% for those exposed to the ad. At the other extreme, exposure to the countervalent message among Republicans likely to vote for Dole decreased support from an average probability of 42% to 37%, holding all other variables constant. This finding raises two important points: First, the consistency in the effect (5% in each case) suggests that the effect of exposure to the countervalent message in this example is purified of confounding influences; and second, it demonstrates the power of the countervalent message in terms of public support for policy initiatives. Even though 5% is not a huge effect, it was of a sufficient magnitude to swing aggregate public opinion from mildly positive to mildly negative.

STUDY TWO: UNDERSTANDING THE EFFECTS OF POLITICAL SOPHISTICATION

In the previous section, a clear finding for the impact of media coverage on policy positions was shown using public opinion data at the aggregate level. The results indicate exposure to the Harry and Louise advertisement decreased support for the Clinton health plan by a consistent 5% across all groups. However, due to the limitations of the data, it was not possible to measure whether health policy sophistication had a mediating impact on the 5% decline. That is, due to limitations of the data used in the previous model, it is not possible to address whether the 5% decline in support is constant across all levels of sophistication, or whether high sophisticates do indeed have stable preferences, while low sophisticates can be influenced by priming.

To address this question, I undertook an experimental examination of media effects on subjects with varying levels of general political sophistication and domain-specific (health policy) sophistication. The sample itself was drawn from the population at Georgia State University in Atlanta, Georgia. Although the sample is not random, it is also not the typical student sample, as Table 6.4 shows. Generally, the sample matched the population of Atlanta (younger, diverse, Democratic) quite well with a plurality of whites (47.8%) and Democrats (47.8%) with an average age of 26. A majority of the respondents were women (52.8%) and most of the respondents described themselves as moderate (39.0%) to liberal (43.4%). In terms of education, there was a variance that one may not expect among a typical student sample, although 64.2% reported having "some college," there was remarkable variance in the remainder of the sample, with 9% reporting either a graduate degree or attendance in a graduate program, 7.5% reported having only a high school diploma, and 17% reported having earned a college degree.

The overall design tested how exposure to the health care story influenced health care policy preferences among other things (see chapter 7 for an additional analysis). The experiment was conducted in December 1999 and January 2000. Participants were told that they were participating in a study of the upcoming political campaign. The subjects were randomly assigned to one of four conditions, a control group (no health care story) or a treatment group where they read about health care. All participants were given three large envelopes numbered 1, 2 and 3 and were instructed to open them in sequential order. The first envelope contained a paper-and-pen survey with various questions drawn from the *National Election Study* interspersed with political sophistication questions based on DelliCarpini and Keeter's (1996) scale and health policy sophistication questions developed with the assistance of Mark Schlesinger. The critical part of the first survey for this anlysis is a section listing the Schlesinger and Lau (2000) health policy metaphors. The metaphors were identified by name and a new category—health care as a public/private partnership—was added for reasons that will become apparent shortly. After rating all of the health policy metaphors in terms of preference, participants were asked to select the metaphor that they would most prefer as a model for health care in the United States.

Once the participants completed the first questionnaire, they were instructed to open envelope number 2. All envelopes contained two stories drawn from local media reports on subjects not directly related to the political campaign (high-speed Internet in Atlanta and a criminal investigation of a local nightclub). In the treatment groups there was a third story on a new health care

TABLE 6.4
Descriptive Statistics for Party Identification, Ideology and Demographics
($N = 159$)

Variable	Percent
Party Identification	
Strong Democrat	16.4%
Weak Democrat	31.4%
Independent	30.2%
Weak Republican	18.2%
Strong Republican	3.8%
Ideology	
Liberal	12.6%
Liberal Leaning	30.8%
Moderate	39.0%
Conservative Leaning	16.4%
Conservative	1.3%
Demographics (Average Age 26 years)	
White	47.8%
African American	38.9%
Asian	4.4%
Hispanic	1.4%
Male	47.2%
Female	52.8%
Education	
High School Graduate	7.5%
Some College	64.2%
College Graduate	17%
Some Graduate School	5%
Graduate Degree	4%

plan (see the Methodological Appendix for a sample of this story) proposed by either Bill Clinton, Al Gore, or Bill Bradley (depending on treatment). The plan was, of course, fictitious and it was crafted so that it fit within the new metaphor health care as a public/private partnership. The participants were instructed to carefully read these stories and upon completion return the stories to their envelope before opening the final envelope.

Envelope number 3 contained a political questionnaire based on the National Election Study, and included candidate-feeling thermometers and questions about the health care metaphors (however, the labels were removed and the metaphors were instead referred to as "options"). The participants were again instructed to rate each of the options and then to select their preferred option for health care in the United States. The preferred options from survey one (pretreatment) were then compared to the preferred options in survey two (posttreatment) to create a "change" variable. Overall, 21.4% of the participants changed their preferences from some other option in the first questionnaire to health care as a public/private partnership in the second questionnaire. In the analysis that follows, I examine whether the change was due to a systematic effect from exposure to the story and whether the effect varied according to subjects' domain-specific sophistication.

The following equations were estimated using a logit model to investigate the effect of media coverage on individuals with varying levels of general political sophistication and domain-specific (health care) sophistication. In these models, *Change* in health care policy preferences is explored as a function of varying levels of general sophistication (*Political Sophistication*) or domain-specific policy sophistication (*Health Care Sophistication*), exposure to the *Treatment* and the *Interaction* between the two, with *Ideology* as a control variable. Specifically, the general political sophistication model is:

$$\text{Change} = \beta_0 + \beta_1 \text{ Political Sophistication} + \beta_2 \text{ Treatment} +$$
$$\beta_3 \text{ Interaction (Political Sophistication * Treatment)} +$$
$$\beta_4 \text{ Ideology} + \mu_2 \qquad (6.2)$$

and, the domain-specific policy sophistication model is:

$$\text{Change} = \beta_0 + \beta_1 \text{ Health Care Sophistication} + \beta_2 \text{ Treatment} +$$
$$\beta_3 \text{ Interaction (Health Care Sophistication * Treatment} +$$
$$\beta_4 \text{ Ideology} + \mu_3 \qquad (6.3)$$

Using these models, I test the effect of exposure to the health story on policy positions as a function of sophistication. Specifically, I analyze how the two types of sophistication (general and domain specific) interact with exposure to the story. With these models, I investigate how information about health care, in the form of a news story, influences the policy positions of citizens with varying degrees of knowledge (see also Gilens, 2001).

DISCUSSION

The results of these estimations are presented in Table 6.5. The findings here indicate mixed yet intriguing results. In equation 6.2, I examine the interaction of general political sophistication and exposure to the media story in the context of preference changes for a health policy metaphor following a priming intervention. There are no effects in this model, although the coefficients are signed as expected—political sophistication is negative, treatment is positive, and the interaction is again negative—they all fail to reach statistical significance. This is surprising; however, when one considers Gilens (2001) work, this is not an unusual result. Recall that Gilens (2001) argues that general political sophistication measures are not refined enough to gauge the impact of issue information on respondents' policy positions. He finds that the level of policy-specific knowledge is an important determinant in how individuals process information and evaluate policies. Nevertheless, this could be viewed as a small sample problem or some other confounding factor were it not for the results in equation 6.3. In that equation, I test the same interaction but with health policy sophistication—that is, domain-specific knowledge—replacing general political sophistication.

The second column in Table 6.5, presents the results for domain-specific sophistication in equation 6.3. Unlike in equation 6.2, there are significant effects for the treatment and for the interaction of the treatment with health policy sophistication. Specifically, those individuals exposed to the health care story (coded against the control group) were more likely to change their health policy preference after reading the treatment story (4.8906). However, the more important finding is that among sophisticates exposed to the story there was a significant negative effect on the likelihood of changing from some other health policy preference to the health policy that was primed. Indeed, among high health policy sophisticates who were exposed to the prime, there is a small (2.1%) likelihood of change. Thus, there is indeed an effect from exposure to the media priming; however, it seems to be substantively ineffective on high sophisticates.

Overall, Table 6.5 presents a compelling argument that policy preferences can be influenced by media priming, as Jacobs and Shapiro (2000) have found. However, the manipulation is not substantially influential among individuals with domain-specific policy knowledge (see Gilens, 2001, for a complementary examination). Finally, while the effects of general and domain-specific sophistication were separated for clarity of discussion, it should be noted that the effects are consistent in the combined model when both sophistication measures are present (see column three of Table 6.5).

Table 6.6 presents a sensitivity analysis to demonstrate how varying levels of health care sophistication affected the likelihood of changing policy preferences following exposure to the health care stories. Table 6.6 presents likelihood of change only for individuals exposed to the treatment story. The sophistication measure itself is normally distributed across a zero to one scale, with a mean of 0.55 and a standard deviation of 0.20. Table 6.6 shows how

TABLE 6.5
Single-Stage Logit Estimations (Change in Health Policy Preference as
Dependent Variable) ($N = 159$)

	Equation 6.2	*Equation 6.3*	*Combined Model*
Political Sophistication	−.7160		−.7057
	(1.6247)		(1.6069)
Health Care Sophistication		2.2848	2.1365
		(3.3636)	(3.3927)
Treatment	1.3792	4.8906**	5.0642*
	(1.4591)	(2.3075)	(2.6935)
Interaction(Political Sophistication* Treatment)	−1.3974		−.6759
	(1.9345)		(1.9805)
Interaction (Health Care Sophistication * Treatment)		−7.5741**	−7.0344*
		(3.7543)	(3.7978)
Ideology	−.1416	−.2791	−.2412
	(.2250)	(.2370)	(.2438)
Constant	−.8180	−2.3422	−1.8376
	(1.4065)	(2.0805)	(2.4519)
	Log Likelihood = −149.884	Log Likelihood = −155.569	Log Likelihood = −139.109
	Percent Correctly Predicted = 80.13	Percent Correctly Predicted = 80.77	Percent Correctly Predicted = 80.77
	Reduction in Error = 26.68	Reduction in Error = 26.47	Reduction in Error = 26.47

*$p < .10$; **$p < .05$.

varying levels of health care sophistication affect the increased probability of changing preferences from some other health care metaphor to the primed metaphor health care as a public/private partnership. Looking across the range of sophistication from zero (answering no questions correctly) to one (answering all questions correctly), the effect of domain-specific policy sophistication on resistance to priming is shown. In this example, the likelihood of changing from some other metaphor to the primed metaphor is 97.6% among low sophisticates, but only 2.1% among high sophisticates. Thus, in spite of the confidence in politicians that their crafted talk will indeed be able to persuade and move public opinion, it is clear that this potential is only present for individuals with nonexistent to moderate domain-specific policy information.

TABLE 6.6
Likelihood of Changing Health Policy Preference With Varying Health
Policy Sophistication Among Members of the Treatment Group

Sophistication	Likelihood
Low (0.00)	97.6%
0.25	86.1%
Medium (0.50)	48.3%
0.75	12.3%
High (1.00)	2.1%

CONCLUSION

At the beginning of this chapter, I set out to investigate under what conditions the media affects audiences, and how those effects influenced health policy positions. My primary concern throughout this book has been to explain policy change within a path dependent context, and to examine how the evolutionary changes in policy that North (1990) describes come about in reality. In this chapter I find that one of the ingredients of change, media coverage, is important and depends on sophistication (see also chapter 5). The exploration included a national survey, examining the impact of a negative media campaign on support for Clinton's health plan. Generally, my results are consistent with other findings on negative media campaigns (Ansolabehere & Iyengar, 1994; Ansolabehere et al., 1994), showing that among individuals exposed to the Harry and Louise advertisement, support for the Clinton health plan decreased by 5% across the board. Thus, it is clear that, as Jacobs and Shapiro (2000) and others assert, the Harry and Louise campaign presents an excellent example of the large role played by the media in policy change. The results in this chapter show that the media had an effect on leading the public away from policy change back to the status quo.

The second part of this chapter deals with the conditions under which the media, like the Harry and Louise campaign, or the crafted talk of President Clinton or other political elites could influence changes in policy preferences. In that study, relying on experimental data, the results indicate that exposure to issue information results in dramatically different effects according to varying levels of domain-specific policy sophistication. However, it is unrelated and unaffected by general political sophistication. Although information exposure was highly likely to lead to changes in health policy preferences, it had little effect on individuals with high levels of domain-specific (health care) policy sophistication.

In the next chapter, the effects of the media are explored further, although from a different perspective. The research and analysis in the next chapter rely on the data used here in chapter 6. However, the view is different in that chapter 7 looks at the effects of exposure to a negative media campaign in association with intentions to vote for presidential candidates who are closely associated with the policy targeted by his/her campaign. The analysis presented in chapter 7 completes the exploration of the elements of policy change in a path dependent system laid out in chapter 2. This is accomplished by coming full circle to examine how policy proposals and the components of the underlying turbulence that are affected by those proposals ultimately related to political candidates.

Chapter 7

Media Effects and Policy Opinions

How "Harry and Louise" Affected
Presidential Vote Intentions

INTRODUCTION

President Clinton's attempt at health care reform was, as I have discussed in previous chapters, an effort to change health care policy in the United States in an evolutionary way. Rather than building incrementally as others had done (Medicare and Medicaid, for example) and as he would do later (State Children's Health Insurance Plan), President Clinton proposed a new health policy that would transform the nature and role of government in health care for generations to come. It seemed that the elements were present for such a change, however, the very tool that Clinton and his aides hoped to use to bring public opinion in line with the proposal—the media—came back to haunt the Clinton health plan and the Clinton administration. In the previous chapter, the impact of the Harry and Louise advertisements was examined in the context of support for the Clinton health plan. The notable finding presented there was that exposure decreased support by 5%, enough to change the outcome. In this chapter, I examine the role that Harry and Louise played as an example of media priming (Jacobs & Shapiro, 2000) in affecting evaluations of Clinton. This was a question on the minds of many. Indeed, Jacobs and Shapiro note that the problems for Clinton went beyond the Harry and Louise advertisements:

The media's shift from national policy to strategic frames presented the public with a steady flow of reports about political posturing, fierce bickering, and uncertainty about the outcome of health care reform. In the wake of this visibly intense partisanship and the media's spotlighting of the ensuing political conflict, there was a noticeable drop in the public's confidence in the Democratic Party to improve health care and its support for the Clinton plan. (p. 235)

Overall, the debate about the Health Security Act was no longer about health security—or even health care for that matter. Instead, it was about politics. The conventional wisdom, at least according to the infamous "Kristol Memo" was that if President Clinton's Health Security Act passed, he would establish a Democratic dynasty built on the HSA, like President Roosevelt's dynasty built on Social Security and the New Deal. Likewise, the logic followed, if the HSA failed, it would represent a significant defeat and could ultimately mean that the Republicans would regain control of the White House in 1996.

Although the Republicans fell short of winning the presidency in 1996, they had an overwhelming victory in 1994, just months after the demise of the Health Security Act. Indeed, in November 1994, the Democrats lost control of both houses of Congress and the losses were the largest ever encountered by the president's party. As Jacobs and Shapiro (2000) note, this was due in large part to the perceived failure of the Clinton administration to do one of the things that they were elected to do—fix health care. Overall, the perception of Clinton (and by association, the Democratic Party) as someone who could do something about health care was tarnished. This was partly because of the media campaign centered around Harry and Louise, in which the Health Security Act was presented as a flawed plan. Of course, as I discussed earlier, the media campaign was wrapped in the context of a political struggle that was about much more than health care. In this chapter, using survey data and an experiment, I examine how this system worked. Specifically, I look at whether negative media coverage about Clinton's health care plan led to downgraded opinions of Clinton's ability to do anything about health care (or other important issues) which in turn led to a further erosion of support for Clinton's plan and in turn Democratic defeats.

MEDIA PRIMING

To understand the role the media plays in the path dependent model of health policy change presented thus far, a discussion of media priming is in order. Specifically, media priming is when an issue that is more prominent in the media is weighted more heavily in people's political judgments (Iyengar, 1991; Jacobs & Shapiro, 2000). In other words, priming refers to the impact of news coverage on the weight assigned to specific issues in making political judgments (Iyengar, 1991, p. 133). Media priming has been thoroughly documented in a number of studies over the past decade (Iyengar & Kinder, 1987; Iyengar et al., 1984; Krosnick & Kinder, 1990). The most firmly established effects are based on evidence that people evaluate the president differently after having been exposed to coverage that emphasizes different policy issues. Citizens change the criteria by which they evaluate the president due to exposure to media coverage of issues like defense, energy, and the economy, or scandals such as the Iran Contra Affair. Media attention to an issue increases the accessibility of the issue in recipients' minds and consequently leads them to consider the issue in their evaluations of the president. In a likewise fashion, I expect that media attention to a timely topic such as the Health Security Act caused priming effects for the president during the 1996 election and, more important for the president's party, in the 1994 election.

Conventional wisdom indicates that priming is based solely on people's use of the accessibility heuristic in making political judgments; that is, they use whatever issue is most salient to form evaluations (Fischoff, Slovic, & Lichtenstein, 1980; Higgins & King, 1981). This suggests that frequent media attention to an issue causes a person to change his/her standards of evaluation to include the issue as a criterion. For example, exposure to media coverage about the economy will lead people to use the economy as an issue by which to evaluate the president in the following years in addition to or instead of some other issue.

Iyengar et al. (1984) conducted two experiments in which they attempted to manipulate issue accessibility by showing subjects simulated television news shows with varying degrees of exposure to the target issue. In the first experiment, there were three levels varying the degree of exposure to the target issue (energy) ranging between no coverage, low (only a few stories dealing with the target issue), and high (many stories discussing energy). After viewing one of the three programs, subjects were asked to evaluate the president's general performance, competence, and integrity. The results showed that subjects in the high-accessibility condition did indeed place a greater emphasis on energy in their evaluations of general presidential performance. In the second experiment, only two levels of accessibility were manipulated, no coverage and some coverage of the target issue, which included defense and inflation in addition to energy. The results for this experiment also showed that exposure to coverage of the issue increased the significance of the issue to viewers' overall judgments of the president. However, issue importance decreased for ratings of the president's competence, and even more for evaluations of integrity.

These studies suggest that media coverage increases the accessibility of an issue and leads to a larger emphasis being placed on it in presidential evaluations, but only when the issue is relevant to the judgment subjects are asked to make. On the other hand, when issues are not deemed important criteria for measuring certain presidential dimensions, they do not have a big impact on final evaluations. In this case, energy, defense, and inflation were not considered as relevant to presidential competence as to his general performance, and not relevant at all to his integrity. They suggest that the types of stories to which subjects were exposed led to the consideration of issues in general performance evaluations of the president, but not judgments of his integrity. Furthermore, they suggest that an entirely different set of issues would be more salient in citizens' evaluations of the president's integrity. Hence, it is not clear how priming affects vote choices in the end if different characteristics are more likely to be influenced depending on the issue being primed.

Edwards, Mitchell, and Welch's (1995) research provides further support for issue priming. More specifically, they examined the influence of presidential performance in the economy and foreign policy in overall judgments about presidential approval. They measured saliency by frequency of media coverage (including television and newspaper reports) and public opinion by 25 national public opinion polls. In conjunction with Iyengar et al.'s (1984) findings in the laboratory, Edwards et al. found that increased media attention to an issue, in this case the economy, led to a greater impact of public perception of the president's handling of the economy on his overall approval rating. They argue that the increased media attention made the issue more salient to citizens, which is why they used the issue in their evaluations.

By using poll data from the 1986 *National Election Study* that was being conducted when the revelation of the Iran Contra Affair came about, Krosnick and Kinder (1990) were able to measure and compare differences in public opinion on President Reagan before and after the highly publicized disclosure. In addition to confirming the effects of priming, the results showed that the higher the degree of correspondence between the news stories that constitute the prime and the opinions that are the target of the priming effect, the larger was the extent of the priming effect. In other words, those who initially were less supportive of Reagan, were more influenced by the news coverage of the Iran Contra Affair and had a bigger impact on their evaluation of Reagan overall. Krosnick and Kinder's findings suggest that prominent media coverage of an issue makes the issue more important to people's judgments. Furthermore, the issue is weighed even more heavily in people's evaluations when the information is consistent with preconceived feelings. This suggests that media priming of an issue will simply enhance already existing attitudes toward the president and, therefore, media attention should simply reinforce predispositions to vote for a candidate, following the on-line model of information processing (Lodge, McGraw, & Stroh, 1989).

In this chapter, I argue that media priming should take place for news coverage of health care issues as it did for energy, the economy, and foreign affairs.

By applying media priming theory to health care policy opinions, I demonstrate how the media is a key factor affecting the "turbulence" in the path dependent model of health care change.

MEDIA COVERAGE AND INFORMATION ABOUT THE HEALTH SECURITY ACT

As I discussed in previous chapters, the 1992 presidential election brought the issue of health care to the forefront of the American political agenda, especially after Harris Wofford's victory in a special Senate election in Pennsylvania. This single event had such relevance that Skocpol (1993) termed it the "focusing event" for health care reform (see also Brown, 1994, p. 198; Jacobs & Shapiro, 2000; Kingdon, 1984). Media coverage of health care problems in the United States, including rising costs and increasing numbers of uninsured, dominated headlines following this event. Overall, health care policy became a highly salient issue (Jacobs & Shapiro, 2000).

Throughout the Clinton presidential campaign, health care remained a top policy issue and when Clinton took office in January 1993, the Health Security Act became the most anticipated presidential policy initiative in more than a decade. President Clinton's first act was to appoint First Lady Hillary Clinton to lead a task force to develop health care legislation that aimed to ensure universal access at low cost while maintaining quality. The work of the task force was the subject of intense media speculation, as the long and oftentimes closed-door meetings with hundreds of advisers continued. Finally, in late September 1993, about four months after the original date the plan was promised, President Clinton presented the newly crafted HSA plan to Congress and the nation in a televised speech. This was followed by a tour of the country by President Clinton during which he promoted the HSA, answering questions in town hall meetings like those he had used during his campaign (for a detailed account of this, see Jacobs & Shapiro, 2000).

As discussed in chapters 5 and 6, there were two sets of early critics of the Clinton plan, the Republican leadership in Congress and conservative political commentators who lambasted it. Both of these groups delivered messages about restricted choice and forced participation in government-sponsored cooperative buying plans. They were joined in their battle by another group, the health care and health insurance industries, led by the Health Insurance Association of America, which echoed the rhetoric of the politicians and pundits in an effective national advertising campaign that reached its peak during the winter of 1993/1994. This campaign was dubbed the "Harry and Louise ads," named for the "ordinary Americans" portrayed in the ads whose fears were similar to those of the two opposition groups (for experimental studies show-ing the effectiveness of simple negative health care advertisements, see Cobb & Kuklinski, 1997).

These ads resonated well with a sector of the American public and accord-ing to West, Heith, and Goodwin (1996) they had the desired negative effect (see also Jacobs & Shapiro, 2000, and the discussion in chapter 6). The HSA ultimately failed without even being brought to the floor of the Senate for a vote. While it was clear that it came to be viewed as the biggest failure of the Clinton administration, the question of interest is whether it had implications for the administration. Specifically, I ask whether this advertisement regarding a policy closely associated with and in fact defining the first two years of the Clinton administration had the power to affect vote intentions for president. Generally, I find that it did.

STUDY ONE: DATA AND METHODS

To examine this question, I turn to a February 1994 *Washington Post* poll. The target population consisted of all adults over the age of 18. There were 511 responses across the vote intention and exposure questions of interest.

As Table 7.1 shows, about 39% of the respondents intended to vote for Clinton in 1996, while 37% intended to vote for Dole. Of the 511 respondents, 210 (about 41%) reported having seen the Harry and Louise ads and thus were exposed to the negative media priming, purified of any elite or party identifica-tion cueing effects that may cloud the reception. Finally, Table 7.1 shows that support for the Health Security Act was at 37%, in concurrence with other

TABLE 7.1

Descriptive Statistics for Variables Used in the Model ($N = 511$)

Variable	Mean	Standard Deviation
Clinton	.39	.49
Dole	.37	.48
Exposure	.41	.49
Support	.37	.48
Interaction (Exposure * Support)	.14	.34
Democrat	.31	.46
Republican	.30	.46
Education	2.82	1.19
Income (in thousands)	40.45	26.52

TABLE 7.2
Comparison Based on Harry and Louise Ad Exposure ($N = 511$)

Variable	Exposed	Not Exposed
Clinton	38%	40%
Dole	42%	31%
Support	40%	67%
Democrat	29%	33%
Republican	33%	25%

Note: Percentages are column

opinion polls taken in February 1994 (Jacobs & Shapiro, 1994, 2000; see also, although earlier, Jacobs, Shapiro, & Schulman, 1993).

Table 7.2 shows the simple bivariate relationship of the effects of exposure to the Harry and Louise advertisement. Among those exposed to the ad, only 40% supported the Health Security Act, compared to 67% of those not exposed to the ad. Additionally, although the partisanship of those exposed and not exposed is roughly similar, the intention to vote for Clinton dropped among those exposed. In contrast, the intention to vote for Dole increased by 11% among those who had been exposed to the ad, compared to those not exposed.

STUDY ONE: A MODEL OF PRIMING EFFECTS ON 1996 PRESIDENTIAL VOTE INTENTIONS

In this chapter, I seek to apply past research on media priming effects (Edwards et al., 1995; Krosnick & Kinder, 1990; Iyengar & Kinder, 1987; Iyengar et al., 1984; Iyengar, Peters, & Kinder, 1982). In studies one and two, I examine media effects to demonstrate the importance of priming of health care for presidential vote intentions. Specifically, I examine the influence of the Harry and Louise advertisement, which negatively portrayed the Health Security Act of 1993 on intentions to vote for President Clinton in the 1996 elections using the following model (descriptions of the variables appear in the Methodological Appendix):

$$\text{Clinton} = \beta_0 + \beta_1 \text{ Exposure} + \beta_2 \text{ Support} + \beta_3 \text{ Exposure}^*$$
$$\text{Support} + \beta_4 \text{ Democrat} + \beta_5 \text{ Republican} + \beta_6 \text{ Income} +$$
$$\beta_7 \text{ Education} + \mu_1 \qquad (7.1)$$

Overall, equation 7.1 presents a model of the effect of the variables of interest, exposure to the Harry and Louise advertisement (*Exposure*), overall support for the Clinton health care plan (*Support*) and the interaction between these two (*Exposure* * *Support*) on intentions to vote for Clinton in 1996 (*Clinton*).

STUDY ONE: RESULTS AND DISCUSSION

This model was estimated using a logistic regression (logit) due to the dichotomous nature of the dependent variable. If the hypothesis about media priming holds true, the expectation is that there will be a significant negative impact on vote intentions for Clinton due to exposure to the Harry and Louise advertisements. I also expect that Support for the Health Security Act and the interaction between these two variables will be significant predictors of vote intentions.

As Table 7.3 shows, the results were much as expected. Exposure to the Harry and Louise advertisement had a significant negative impact on intention to vote for Clinton, demonstrating the existence of media priming for long term vote intentions. Additionally, the other variables of interest, Support and the interaction term, performed as expected. Both were highly significant and positive, fitting well with the priming literature. The phenomenon captured by the interaction term shows the impact for those individuals predisposed to support the Health Security Act who were also exposed to the ads.

TABLE 7.3
Logistic Regression Results with Likelihood of Clinton
Vote as Dependent Variable ($N = 511$)

Variable	β	SE
Exposure	−0.60*	.33
Support	1.97***	.38
Interaction (Exposure * Support)	1.09**	.52
Democrat	1.57***	.29
Republican	−1.79***	.39
Income	0.01	.01
Education	−0.01	.12
Constant	−1.42**	.39
−2Log Likelihood = 461.768		
Improvement = 69.8%		

*$p < .10$. **$p < .05$. ***$p < .001$.

Table 7.4
Likelihood of Clinton Vote at Varying Parameter Values

Exposed	Support	Interaction	Democrat	Republican	Likelihood
No	Yes	No	Yes	No	96%
Yes	Yes	Yes	Yes	No	89%
No	No	No	Yes	No	54%
Yes	No	No	Yes	No	52%
No	Yes	No	No	Yes	46%
Yes	Yes	Yes	No	Yes	21%
No	No	No	No	Yes	4%
Yes	No	No	No	Yes	4%

Thus, the interaction term acts as a control to tease out the pure effects of exposure on those not inclined to support the president.

Table 7.4 presents a sensitivity analysis that portrays an excellent means of demonstrating this effect. Reading across the table, eight categories of individuals are shown, with varying exposure and support measures as well as varying partisanship. The final column shows the increased likelihood of intending to vote for Clinton in 1996 based on these parameters. The most interesting effects are among Republican supporters of the Health Security Act. Among this group, exposure to the Harry and Louise advertisement decreased the likelihood of voting for Clinton in 1996 by 25%. This is indeed the most significant finding for media priming on vote intentions. Further, the effect is present even for Democrats who are predisposed to support the Democratic president. Democrats who support the Health Security Act and were exposed to the ad are 7% less likely to vote for Clinton in 1996 than were their counterparts who were not exposed to the ad. This finding is also quite significant given that the 7% decline occurs even in the presence of the control exerted by the interaction term. Thus, exposure to the Harry and Louise advertisement exhibited the classic effects of media priming on a measure of long-term consequence, vote intentions for president.

STUDY TWO: AN EXPERIMENTAL TEST OF MEDIA PRIMING OF HEALTH CARE IN THE 2000 PRESIDENTIAL RACE

In the previous section, I show that the Harry and Louise media message demonstrated a priming effect on presidential vote intentions. In this section, using an experimental design, I seek to examine whether a single newspaper story could prime feelings about presidential candidates in the 2000 election. During the 2000 presidential election primary season, the Democrats (Al Gore and Bill Bradley) turned more attention to health care issues than the Republican candidates. Bill Bradley was most closely associated with proposing sweeping changes to the health care system in a way similar to that of Clinton's Health Security Act.[1] The theory was that subjects exposed to a simulated news story on health care would be primed to think about the candidate who, at the time of the experiment, was most associated with such a proposal, Bill Bradley.

STUDY TWO: DATA AND METHODS

To test this hypothesis, I conducted an experiment at Georgia State University from December 9, 1999, to January 21, 2000. There were 159 subjects in total. (See chapter 6 for additional details of the experiment.) Recall, subjects were randomly assigned to a treatment group ($N = 119$) where they were asked to read a newspaper story about a health care plan proposal that would create a public/private partnership in lieu of a national health insurance plan or a control group ($N = 40$).[2] After reading the story, subjects were asked to answer questions about various political topics and demographic information. Among these questions, subjects were asked their partisanship, ideology, and feeling-thermometer ratings of the major presidential candidates. A summary of this data is presented in Tables 7.5 and 7.6.

Overall, as Table 7.5 shows, 47.8% of the respondents were Democrats, 30.2% were Independent, and 22% were Republicans. In terms of ideology, about 43.4% were liberal and 17.7% considered themselves conservative. Likewise, Table 7.6 shows that the sample was slightly more favorable toward the major Democratic candidates than the Republican candidates with Gore and Bradley scoring 54 and 53, respectively, while Bush and McCain were rated at 48 and 53, respectively.

A MODEL OF PRIMING EFFECTS ON CANDIDATE EVALUATIONS

In this study, I revisit the media-priming hypothesis using experimental data. Recall that the purpose is to determine whether media attention to health care influences evaluations of the candidate associated with the issue. That is, would a newspaper story have the same effect on ratings of Bradley as the Harry and Louise campaign did on evaluations of Clinton. Specifically, I examine whether exposure to a story about a new health care plan based on a public/private partnership influences feelings toward the candidate most

TABLE 7.5
Frequencies for Party Identification, Ideology and
Demographics (*N* = 159)

Variable	Percent
Party Identification	
Strong Democrat	16.4
Weak Democrat	31.4
Independent	30.2
Weak Republican	18.2
Strong Republican	3.8
Ideology	
Liberal	12.6
Liberal Leaning	30.8
Moderate	39.0
Conservative Leaning	16.4
Conservative	1.3
Demographics (Average Age 26 years)	
White	47.8
African American	38.9
Asian	4.4
Hispanic	1.4
Male	47.2
Female	52.8
Education	
High School Graduate	7.5
Some College	64.2
College Graduate	17
Some Graduate School	5
Graduate Degree	4

associated with national health care at the time of the study—Bill Bradley versus Al Gore—the other democratic candidate who did not emphasize health care in the primaries. To test this hypothesis, I developed two models of media priming predicting ratings of the two democratic candidates:

$$FTBradley = \beta_0 + \beta_1 MediaExposure + \beta_2 HealthCare +$$
$$\beta_3 MediaExposure * HealthCare + \beta_4 Ideology + \mu_1 \qquad (7.2)$$

TABLE 7.6
Descriptive Statistics for Feeling Thermometers ($N = 159$)

Variable	Mean	Standard Deviation
Clinton	57	30
Gore	54	26
Bradley	53	17
Bush	48	23
McCain	53	18
Democrats	61	24
Republicans	44	23
Insurance Industry	38	21
Doctors	61	23

$$\text{FTGore} = \beta_0 + \beta_1 \text{MediaExposure} + \beta_2 \text{HealthCare} + \beta_3 \text{MediaExposure} * \text{HealthCare} + \beta_4 \text{Ideology} + \mu_1 \quad (7.3)$$

The expectation was that media priming would take place for Bradley but not for Gore. Increasing accessibility of the health care issue to subjects in the treatment group should influence evaluations of Bradley because it was one of his main campaign issues, whereas it should not influence evaluations of Gore because he was not campaigning on health care at the time.

STUDY TWO: RESULTS AND DISCUSSION

The models were estimated using ordinary least squares regression. If the hypothesis about media priming holds true, the expectation is that there would be a statistically significant and positive effect for holding liberal health care opinions and being primed with the health care story. Specifically, the expectation is that these effects would be present for the candidate associated with health care. Thus, I anticipate priming effects for Bradley because he emphasized health care issues as part of his platform early on in the campaign and before the primaries.[3] On the other hand, I did not expect the health care prime to influence ratings of Gore because at this point in the campaign he had not developed his position on health care as a central part of his platform in the way that Bradley had.

As Tables 7.7 and 7.8 show, the results fall in line with the hypotheses. Media priming took place for Bradley but not for Gore. In other words, reading the health care story did not influence feeling-thermometer ratings of

TABLE 7.7

Ordinary Least Squares Regression Results with Bradley Feeling-Thermometer
($N = 159$) as Dependent Variable

Variable	β	SE
MediaExposure	-32.68**	10.90
HealthCare	30.56**	16.00
Interaction (MediaExposure * Health Care)	54.23**	17.50
Ideology	-2.921**	1.44
Constant	79.08***	11.40
$R^2 = .11$		

**$p < .05$. ***$p < .001$.

TABLE 7.8

Ordinary Least Squares Regression Results with Gore Feeling-Thermometer
as Dependent Variable ($N = 159$)

Variable	β	SE
MediaExposure	2.8	15.84
HealthCare	43.70*	23.32
Interaction (MediaExposure * HealthCare)	-7.09	25.41
Ideology	-7.60***	2.10
Constant	49.10***	16.56
$R^2 = .19$		

*$p < .10$. **$p < .05$. ***$p < .001$.

Gore, which were in line with my expectations because Gore was not yet pushing his health care platform.

On the other hand, exposure to the health care story had a significant negative impact on feelings toward Bradley among subjects who held conservative
health care opinions ($\beta = -32.68; p < .05$). Feeling-thermometer ratings of
Bradley decreased as a result of subjects reading about health care when they
held conservative views, despite the fact that the story proposed a public/private
partnership. Conversely, the effect of Media Exposure among respondents
with liberal health care opinions had a significant positive effect on feeling-
thermometer ratings of Bradley ($\beta = 30.56, p < .05$). In other words, exposure

to the simulated news story increased evaluations of Bradley among respondents who also held liberal positions on health care, and likewise decreased assessments among subjects who held conservative positions on health care. Thus, I show that media priming of health care caused vote intentions for Bradley to change in a controlled laboratory environment. Hence, coupled with my findings for Clinton in the real world, it appears that media priming of health care influences political evaluations as well as vote intentions.

CONCLUSION

Overall, it appears that media priming increases the importance of health care opinions in subjects' evaluations of presidential candidates who are perceived as affiliated with the issue. Study One shows how exposure to the Harry and Louise advertisements about the Clinton aministration's Health Security Act affected the likelihood of expressing an intention to vote for Clinton in 1996. Among respondents who supported the HSA, reporting exposure to the ad increased intentions to vote for Clinton. In Study Two, I explored the same theory using an experimental approach in which exposure to the media message is controlled. Again, the findings indicate that media priming took place. Reading about health care caused health care opinions to significantly influence favorability ratings of presidential candidate Bill Bradley, but not his counterpart Al Gore. This suggests that media attention to health care only influences evaluations of political actors who are associated with health care (Iyengar et al., 1984). Generally speaking, it appears that media communication about health care not only serves to inform citizens of the policies and issues at hand but also acts as an instrument by which Americans evaluate political candidates (Jacobs & Shapiro, 2000).

Although we know that President Clinton did go on to be elected to a second term and was able to increase his margin, polling nearly 50% of the vote in the three-candidate race, some may argue that the media coverage of health care did not carry over, in that Clinton was elected to a second term in 1996. However, that argument is tempered by the fact that in the midterm elections in 1994, just nine months after this poll was conducted, the Democrats lost control of both houses of Congress by greater margins than any previous incumbent party. During this time, the Health Security Act was still salient, having been tabled in the Senate only three months earlier. This election was viewed as a referendum on the Clinton presidency and was, according to some, the final chapter in the story of the Health Security Act. Thus, there is evidence that these long-term vote intentions may have been carried out at the next possible opportunity to cast a vote on President Clinton, while the "bad" policy that defined his presidency was still accessible in the minds of the electorate (see Jacobs & Shapiro, 2000, for an in-depth discussion of this concept). While it is impossible to say with certainty that the negative perceptions of Clinton, generated by the Harry and Louise ad campaign, were linked to this 1994 election result, there appears to be some evidence to support the existence of media priming of health care influencing political evaluations and vote intentions.

Overall, coupled with the previous chapter, the results here show the powerful impact of the media on policy proposals and as a result on policy change. This represents a new perspective on past studies of media priming, by modeling the effects of exposure to a negative media campaign on intentions to vote for a president closely associated with the policy targeted by the campaign. In this chapter, I demonstrated that exposure to the Harry and Louise advertisements geared against the Clinton administration's Health Security Act dramatically decreased the likelihood of expressing an intention to vote for Clinton in 1996.

This was true for Democrats, even in the presence of a strong control for preexisting vote intentions, and especially for Republicans who were inclined to support the Health Security Act. This finding suggests that voter information campaigns can be extremely important to generating support or opposition for policies. As with the findings in chapter 6, the results in this chapter suggest that media campaigns can have effects on political behavior that are long term and affect more than approval ratings. Further, media campaigns, like Harry and Louise and the coverage of health care reform during this period that Jacobs and Shapiro (2000) discuss, have the power to prevent policy change in favor of the status quo. As the evidence presented shows, the Harry and Louise · media coverage affected perceptions of President Clinton as a leader. Further, as Jacobs and Shapiro (2000) suggest, the ability of the Democratic Party to address the complex issues of health care was called into question. Whether this is the sole reason for the resounding defeat of the Democratic Party in the 1994 midterm elections is questionable. However, it is a virtual certainty that the downgraded evaluations of President Clinton and the ultimate failure of the long-awaited Clinton plan for health care reform were factors in that process. In this case, although the elements seemed to be present for health care reform, public support was swayed and the turbulence that had once been present calmed to reveal the status quo as the preferred health policy in the United States. This is an idea that is explored further in the next and final chapter.

Chapter 8

Dynamic Health Policy Change

A Cohesive Approach

INTRODUCTION

In the preceding chapters, the premise was that in order to understand policy change, it is necessary to understand the environment in which policy develops. However, as Lippmann (1965) noted, this environment is at times, "too complex" (p. 11). Others such as Kingdon (1984), Baumgartner and Jones (1993), and Skocpol (1993) echo Lippman's sentiment. The difficulty, and indeed the challenge, for most of us is to understand the complexity of the policy system and politics in general. Given that, the question is How should we conceive the complexity? Beyond that, if we can indeed understand the complexity of policy change, what are the implications?

It is not enough to simply say that the policy system is complex—that statement simply introduces the groundwork for a tautology—policy is complex because it arises in a complex environment and the environment is complex because policy is complex. Rather, it is necessary to deconstruct the complexity, as Lippmann (1965) suggested so that it can be reconstructed with greater understanding. By first using Occam's razor to pare the study of policy change into its component parts, one can then reconstruct policy change with greater understanding. In this book, I have suggested that one way to understand the complexities of policy change is to look at a representative policy area—in this case, health care. However, simply choosing a policy area is not enough, because even in tearing down a complex environment, there must be a framework upon which the levels of understanding can be reconstructed. In this book, I used path dependence, which is well established in the literature

125

(North, 1990; Wilsford, 1994), as a framework for understanding health care policy in general. I then note that the complexity of the system is most visible during times of policy change. Thus, to understand policy change, it is necessary to understand the components of the complex environment within which changes in policy occur.

In a path dependent system, the events that occur—changes in policy— advance in a cause-and-effect manner (because this happens, that will happen). Indeed, in some systems, it is possible that the entire development of policy proceeds that way. In fact, before Medicare and Medicaid, health policy in the United States proceeded in that fashion, advancing slowly over time without any defining evolutionary advances. However, it is also possible, within a path dependent system that policy will advance in an evolutionary way (North, 1990), that is, a way in which there is such dramatic change that the policy which existed only months or days before is recognizable only as an ancestor, not a direct predecessor, of the new policy. The events that lead to such a change are the very nature of complexity in the policy system. The forces of change or potential for change are impermanent, that is, the window of opportunity (Baumgartner & Jones, 1993) for change exists only briefly. Of course, there are, as I have discussed, times when change appears imminent, but does not occur (the Health Security Act, for example). In these cases, the elements of change are present, but because they are impermanent and subject to manipulation, change does not occur and the turbulence that is so important to evolutionary changes in policy calms until a cause for change arises again. To summarize, there are three necessary conditions for evolutionary change in a path dependent system: a cause for change, conditions that can support change (which are by nature impermanent), and a cause and conditions that correlate with the intended effect of the change.

I have relied on this premise to explore policy change in health care by deconstructing a complex system into its component parts to add greater understanding to the cause for policy change, the support for policy change, and the intentions of policy change. In some cases, these have come together to change health care policy permanently (Medicare and Medicaid) and in others they have not (the HSA and other attempts to enact a universal coverage system). A key component in the construction of a model of policy change within a path dependent system is public opinion in its various forms. In fact, one way to summarize this book would be to say that it is about public opinion and health care policy change. Indeed, there is support for that description in that I examined how public attitudes and the beliefs of elites influenced health care policy. Along with this, I examined what halts change—that is, how the impact of path dependence and other contextual factors affect health care policy evolution. Recall that path dependence, as it is used in this book, relies on North's (1990) notion of institutions that can change either through creation or evolution. Much of his research is dedicated to the notion of path dependence, which is an evolutionary perspective on changing institutions. North argues that policy change, as defined by institutional change, is incremental. In his view, institutions are, on the surface, stable. However, "from conventions, codes of conduct, and norms of behavior to statute law, and common law, and contracts between individuals, institutions are evolving and therefore, are continually altering the choices available to us" (p. 6). This is the essence of path dependence—institutions evolve slowly over time. Thus, having only a cause for change is not sufficient to achieve policy change. For example, the fact that at any given time approximately 40 million Americans are uninsured may be a valid cause for changing health care policy. However, it is not the case that a cause alone can produce change. Nor is it sufficient that the proposed change will affect the cause—with universal health care, the uninsured Americans would have health care coverage. Instead, the link between cause and effect must pass through and maintain the conditions to support the change. This is what North refers to as the "turbulence underlying the policy system" and it is the component that is most complex. For that reason, understanding the conditions that both promote and deter changes in policy has been the primary goal of this book.

To do this, I have examined policy change within a four-part system of causality that breaks the complexity down into component parts. The first examines how forces of nature, as a game theorist uses the term *nature*, affects the possibility of change. This is the reason for the underlying path dependent structure in that path dependence represents natural progression of policy. The second lies in efficacy, that is, the way that the nature of a system provides the capacity for change. In this case, the nature of a path dependent system allows for changes that are either incremental (slowly evolving) or dynamic (rapidly changing) within a stable institutional structure. Although this is a recurrent theme, chapter 3 was most devoted to this element of causality. The third component is an examination of how dependent relationships transform the policy debate. By dependent relationships, I mean the dependence of results on events; that is, how policy change is influenced, promoted, or deterred, based on the environment in which the potential for change arises. This is the theme in many of the chapters. For example, in chapter 4, the role of the president as an advocate for health policy change addressed this very concept. How can the president change policy given myriad environmentally defining characteristics that all have within them the possibility to promote or prevent change? In chapter 5, this idea was again addressed by examining how characteristics of the citizens (policy sophistication) influenced the possibility for policy change. Finally, chapters 6 and 7 examined how the media contributes to this process, both in terms of policy support and support for the president.

The fourth component ties all of this together by looking back on the developments for proof of validity of the cause for policy change. To borrow again from game theorists, this is much like backward induction, in that it requires that the result be used to explain how the cause and effect developed. This is a unique way of opening the black box of policy change because it looks to the end result and then requires that one trace that back through the complexity to understand why policy changed, or alternatively, why a policy change failed. For example, in chapter 3, I explored how changes in the social constructions of the elderly coupled with a more liberal mood among the American public resulted in the passage of Medicare. In chapter 4, I again addressed this concept by comparing and contrasting the success of Medicare and Medicaid with the failure of the Health Security Act. Chapter 4, then, set the stage for the analyses of the Health Security Act that followed. All of these analyses were grounded in the quest for proof of validity. That is to say, if the Health Security Act did in fact have a cause—40 million uninsured Americans or escalating costs or some other reason—then the result should have been passage. However, within the black box of policy, there was a breakdown in the conditions of support for change. This is an idea addressed at length by Jacobs and Shapiro (2000) and it was the central focus of chapters 5, 6, and 7 of this book. In these chapters, the failure of the HSA—the result—was examined within the context of public opinion as a function of sophistication and media forces. In the end, it is clear that the failure of the HSA was not because the cause was not valid, but rather because of the breakdown of support for the Clinton plan.

The components of the HSA's demise may very well have been in the fact that it violated the nature of the path dependent system, without enough support to overcome the violation and create a truly evolutionary change in policy. Clinton's attempt at health care reform was, as I have discussed in previous chapters, an effort to change health care policy in the United States in an evolutionary way. It was, in every way, an evolutionary change in policy. Rather than building incrementally as even the quasi-evolutionary Medicare and Medicaid plans had done, and as Clinton eventually did with his State Children's Health Insurance Plan, Clinton proposed an entirely new system with the HSA. Indeed, President Clinton proposed a new health policy that would transform the nature and role of government in health care for generations to come. Although it seemed, at the time, that the elements were present for such a change, clearly, as the backward induction in the quest for validity of the cause for health policy change, they were not.

Thus, policy change can be examined in terms of three components: causes for change, conditions for change, and the correlation of the two. Further, when policy can or does change, it can be examined by looking at four elements: the nature of the system, the possibility for efficacy, the dependent relationships within the system, and the validity of the proposal. Together, these provide tools to examine policy change. The remaining component—context—is integrated with these tools, but remains distinct. Context is somewhat less amorphous, in that context is defined easily, as the values and ideologies of the public and the elites based on available information. Thus, while institutions define path dependence, context is defined by identifiable, but impermanent, factors such as knowledge, power, and motivations of actors in the political environment as well as variables that define the attitudes of those actors. Together, these ideas—context and path dependency— effectively model the characteristics of the decision setting.

The previous chapters represent a series of snapshots of health care policy and health care policy change. I used this method to break down the complex policy arena of health care into manageable components. Overall, this book demonstrates that health care policy in the United States is the product of the activities of a number of actors at various levels, ranging from the typical voter to the president. The major conclusion drawn from this work is that change in health care policy can occur rapidly or advance slowly and incrementally, depending on context. That is, even in a system that is by its nature path dependent, there are times when conditions align and evolutionary policy change is the result. The question is What are the implications of the knowledge and understanding gleaned from the deconstruction of policy change?

THE PUBLIC MOOD AND NATIONAL HEALTH CARE SPENDING

In chapter 3, the mediating effect of public mood on federal health care policy was explored. The data presented in chapter 3 showed the mediating and predictive impact of public mood on federal health care expenditures (see also Jacobs and Shapiro, 2000). The relationship itself seems quite obvious, as the public becomes more liberal in its attitudes, federal health care spending increases. This is undoubtedly the case across all social programs when the mood is more liberal; people are more likely to support liberal policy agendas by a margin sufficient to make their pursuit worthwhile to politicians seeking reelection (Erickson, McIver, & Wright, 1993; Stimson, 1999). However, the discussion in chapter 3 steps back from this simple relationship in the data to explain how public opinion, the ultimate influence on health care spending, was, in fact, influenced by political rhetoric. The discussion of the social construction of elderly populations shows an example of how politicians and interest groups were able to shape public opinion so that there would be support for the Medicare program (Koff & Park, 1999).

The analysis presented in chapter 3 also provides some insight into the failure of the Health Security Act. Although the American public had become more liberal in the decade leading up to the HSA, there was not a significant enough majority to make pursuit of a large government program attractive enough to election-minded politicians. It is quite probable that the failure to move public opinion in support of the HSA was not only President Clinton's fault, but also a function of the opinion-shaping rhetoric of Republican elites and interest groups (see, for example, Jacobs and Shapiro, 2000). In the end, the lesson to be learned is that the politics of policy change requires the underlying support of the public. That is to say, the public must be predisposed to the type of policy change that is being proposed. In conservative times, no matter how well intentioned or well thought out, a liberal policy change will not succeed. However, in chapter 4, I explored whether a well-presented liberal policy change could succeed in conservative times. The question there was whether an entrepreneurial president could persuade the public to support and the Congress to adopt his preferred policy, regardless of the mood.

HEALTH POLICY HISTORY AND PRESIDENTIAL ACTIVITY

The analysis presented in chapter 4 was wrapped within a modern history of federal health care policy through an examination of presidential-level initiatives. This is perhaps the most direct examination of politics and national health care policy because it discusses the role of a political elite, the president, in crafting health care policy. Overall, four presidents—Truman, Kennedy, Johnson, and Clinton—actively pursued national health care reform with varying degrees of success. The ability of these presidents to achieve dynamic health policy change was tempered by the political environment in which they operated. The data presented in chapter 4 showed how factors exogenous to the policy area itself create boundaries and thereby shape the nature of the policy change itself. At times, these boundaries prevent change entirely, while at other times change occurs, but only incrementally. Of course, the central theme was whether the president could influence any of this debate.

The conclusion was that the president influences the process, either as an active participant shaping the policy outputs or as a bystander watching policy advance incrementally without active interference. All of this takes place within the political arena, which is shaped, bounded, and tempered in many ways by the public: their mood and their preferences. In the traditional understanding of presidential power, the chief executives use speeches and other discussions of health care policy to try to mold this opinion so that their policies may be enacted. Their success or failure of the crafted talk (Jacobs & Shapiro, 2000) depends on myriad factors that set the context of the debate, and the ultimate fate of their proposals, as the following chapters showed, depends in great part on public opinion. The lesson to be taken away from chapter 4 is that presidents can indeed persuade, as Neustadt (1990) noted long ago. However, that ability and the success of the president in his efforts depend on the context in which the action takes place. There are indeed myriad factors that define context and thus define the policy space. These constraints, in turn, dictate what action the president and other elites can take to move policy. Overall, understanding this process goes far in advancing our understanding of why so much policy change is incremental.

THE RISE AND THE DEMISE OF THE HEALTH SECURITY ACT

Chapters 5, 6, and 7 addressed the question that chapter 4 left unanswered in regard to the Health Security Act. The nagging question in regard to the Health Security Act, especially to one who believes that the public is rational is How could the Health Security Act fail when it promised to give people everything they said they wanted in poll after poll and focus group after focus group? Jacobs and Shapiro (2000) provide one answer, stating that rather than providing what the public wanted, it provided what the Clinton administration wanted the public to want. They develop the innovative concept of crafted talk to explain how this happened. In the analyses presented in chapters 5, 6, and 7, all of which are linked by the common explanation of information, I probed further into this notion.

Chapter 5 presented a study of the role of policy-specific knowledge on support for a policy. In that chapter, the role of competing information flows provided a context for examining how accurate information held by the public was used to develop policy attitudes toward the HSA. The question addressed was whether people who had all of the relevant information about the HSA, that is, people who knew that the HSA provided what they said they wanted, acted rationally and supported the act. The data showed clearly that people more knowledgeable about the details of the Health Security Act were much more likely to support it. This finding is important because the general consensus was that the HSA failed, because it was so complex (West, Heith, & Goodwin, 1996) that most people did not realize it featured components they said they wanted (but see Jacobs & Shapiro, 2000). Thus, the HSA failed because of its complexity and the failure of the president and his surrogates to convince the public that the Health Security Act was indeed the plan that the public had requested. A lesson for politicians that comes from this analysis is that simplicity must be the mantra for anyone who would seek to change policy. This is because a simple policy allows for a simple message. With a simple message, opponents may be less likely to obfuscate the nature of the policy proposal.

Indeed, the chief problem for the Clinton plan was in the information and misinformation of crafted talk. In chapter 6, I examined the role and power of misinformation in affecting support for the Health Security Act at the margins through an analysis of the "Harry and Louise" advertising campaign. Generally, the data showed a 5% across-the-board decrease in support for the Health Security Act among those exposed to the Harry and Louise advertisements. While this effect may seem small, in reality, it was more than enough to defeat the plan. Consider, for example, how a poll showing 47% support among the American public versus a poll showing 52% would influence the decisions of the members of Congress deciding whether or not to vote for the HSA. (Indeed, many elections are won and lost on margins generally much smaller than 5%.) Further, the experimental evidence presented in chapter 6 shows that attitudes are more resistant to media messages among those with high domain-specific (health care) policy knowledge.

Chapter 7 continued this discussion by examining the impact of Harry and Louise on vote intentions. In this case, the impact is much more dramatic than the findings in chapter 6 and the results provided a plausible explanation for the reluctance of many politicians, especially Democrats, to support the HSA in the end. Overall, the likelihood of voting for Bill Clinton and by surrogate other Democrats among people who were exposed to the Harry and Louise advertisements decreased significantly. This shows the negative impact of association with the HSA for politicians and goes far in explaining not only the abandonment of the Health Security Act in August 1994, but also, to some extent, the disastrous results for the Democrats in the 1994 elections. The findings in both chapters 6 and 7 are supported with experimental data. The confirmatory results clearly show the impact of media coverage on changing policy opinions among less sophisticated individuals, as well as the power of media coverage to influence vote choice.

In the end, the important lesson from this trio of chapters is that while policy ideas matter, the ideas about policies matter more. That is to say, that what people perceive about a policy and its implications for them may be more important in many ways than the reality of the policy and what it means for them. For elites who seek to change policy, these are indeed important lessons. Information is powerful and the ability to present information in a light that is favorable for the policy proposal is important to policy success. Control of the policy agenda can come from a variety of sources. One of these, is of course the "bully pulpit," however, as the analyses in chapters 5, 6, and 7 showed, that may not be enough. Rather, having control of the message—that is, control of information and, more important, the public perception of a policy—is far more important. At times, as the research in this book has shown, control of the bully pulpit and control of the policy agenda coincide, but far more often—especially with the increasing propensity for divided government—they do not. The advice for those who seek policy change is to pursue changes that are easily explained with straightforward components that can be easily defined. Thus, it would seem that incremental policy change would have the greatest opportunity for success barring a groundswell of support for a dynamic change.

CONCLUSION

The goal of this book was to examine whether public opinion mediates policy outcomes in a specific policy area, health care. To examine that question, I used existing theories of policy change as a basis, discussing the debate between proponents of dynamic policy change and those who believe that incrementalism is the proper explanation. In sum, I showed that both schools of thought may be equally applicable, depending on the mediating role that public opinion plays. It is true that a policy which enjoys enormous public support may be enacted without any need to take incremental steps along the way, the dynamic view. Nevertheless, it is also true that policies with little support among the public or within complex policy areas may be advanced only incrementally. For example, the Health Security Act failed; however, many of its very popular components passed without trouble.

From that statement, it may be tempting to conclude that broad sweeping policy change or expensive policy change is more likely to be subjected to incrementalism. However, an examination of past and present policies shows that is not the case. For example, the 1986 revision of tax policy, like its 2001 counterpart, passed swiftly and with little opposition. However, smaller changes that are essentially costless like campaign finance reforms have languished because of their complexity and the ease in which misinformation can be disseminated about the legislation.

Thus, the true question for policy researchers interested in examining the debate over dynamism versus incrementalism is What role does the public play at the margins? In the studies presented in this book, there is clear evidence that whether a health policy advances in a dynamic manner is subject to the context in which the policy is proposed. Myriad factors that include elite messages, the complexity of the policy, the knowledge of the public about the policy, the nature of media coverage, and the general mood of the public toward federal spending, in turn, define the context. Each of these variables changes under differing circumstances, and their changeability is what makes it impossible to determine in advance whether a policy will advance incrementally or be approved in totality in a single piece of legislation. This is not to say that the outcome of policy is random. Rather, the outcome can be predicted in advance, with a great degree of certainty, if one knows the nature of the variables defining the context. Thus, by February 1994, it would have been safe to assume that the Health Security Act would fail because by that time the variables defining the context had been set. The plan was too complex and it was the subject of intense opposition through elite messages and the media and an increasingly conservative mood among the public. In contrast, the variables defining context while Medicare was being considered point to quick passage, in a dynamic sense.

The overall lesson for policy scholars and policy practitioners is that context matters. As Page and Shapiro (1992) assert, the public is rational, thus when their actions seem irrational, we must examine the circumstances under which these actions take place. In this book, I focused on health care policy and devoted much of the analysis and discussion to the most recent major health policy initiative, the Health Security Act. Nevertheless, the theories, concepts, and methods used here to analyze health care policy can be extended to other domestic policy domains such as tax policy, trade policy, and welfare policy.

Methodological Appendix

INTRODUCTION

As you have seen, the data presented in this book vary considerably and the methods used to analyze the data are equally diverse. The guiding rule in performing the analyses presented was to employ the appropriate method for the data at hand. As a result, in many of the chapters, the analyses are fairly complex statistical estimation procedures or research designs. Thus, some of the methods used are new to political science, policy studies, and public opinion. As the discussions in the text show, the results can be easily interpreted to provide answers to the questions posed. Nevertheless, for those readers who desire a greater discussion of the mechanics involved in the methodology, I have constructed this appendix. In the sections that follow, I elaborate on the various research designs and statistical models used in chapters 3–7. It is my hope that readers not only will gain greater understanding of the analyses presented in the body of the text, but also will be able to adapt the procedures used here to answer questions that interest them.

CHAPTER 3 METHODS

In terms of methodology, the book starts with chapter 3 and, methodologically, chapter 3 is a chapter about time series analysis. The data used in this chapter are time series in the classic sense in that they are a series of observations of the same phenomenon over a period of years. Because this type of time series data is unique, it requires the use of specialized methods. (In contrast, in chapter Four, a cross-sectional pooled time series data set is assembled, and, as you will see, that can be analyzed much like a normal data set, provided a few methodological controls are applied.) Specifically, the data in chapter 3 are based on annual measures of federal spending and public opinion. Generally speaking, this classic type of time series is described in terms of what is happening in the observations in an acronym called ARIMA.

ARIMA Models

ARIMA stands for the three things that can be observed in a time series: autoregressive, integrated, and moving average. The autoregressive portion (AR) refers to the dependence of the current observation on the observation(s) preceding it. That is to say, the AR process takes into account the history of the series. The "I" refers to the changes in the system that occur due to shocks in the form of what is generally referred to as an "intervention." An intervention can be thought of as anything that changes the time series from the path it would have followed as a simple autoregressive process. Finally, the moving average (MA) describes a system that changes in a cyclical fashion.

One way to test for the processes at work in a given system is to create a graph comprised of autocorrelations and partial autocorrelations. Looking at the time series (ARIMA) estimations for the entire series of observations from 1960 to 1999 for the data used in chapter 3, it is apparent from the autocorrelation function and the partial autocorrelation function that there is a significant effect only at the first lag. This means that the change in health care expenditures series and the percent of total health care spending by the federal government are both AR (1) processes where the long-term effect of previous changes on the present change decays exponentially. This fits well within the path dependent nature of the system in that the best predictor of the present federal health care spending is last year's federal health care spending. Further, the estimation results show that the residuals are white noise. This means that the relationship is indeed captured in an AR model and there is little else that can explain the changes in spending that are observed. In short, this analysis indicates that federal health care spending fits well within the path dependent paradigm.

The "I" component is also interesting in terms of the data used in chapter 3. Recall that "I" refers to a shock to the system that changes the observations from their expected path (in this case AR (1)). Like all statistical studies, it is important to fit a model to the data that accurately captures the process. When modeling an intervention, we have four different types of models at our disposal: gradual temporary, gradual permanent, abrupt temporary, and abrupt permanent. These describe the nature of the change in the series. Specifically, the gradual models refer to a change in the series that occurs over time. These look like a hill, going from a lower level to a higher level. In contrast, the abrupt models refer to changes that occur rapidly, in which the series moves instantaneously from one level to another. Likewise, the notions of permanent and temporary refer to what happens after the intervention. A permanent change means that the series never returns to the same levels as before the intervention, while temporary means that there is a rapid return to the preintervention levels. The question thus turns to whether this intervention can be modeled, and whether the effect is significant when it is modeled. To understand this, the process must first be identified; as Norpoth (1987) notes, "what may appear gradual with monthly measures, may look abrupt with quarterly measures" (p. 7). In chapter 3, the first method employed is an intervention analysis where the adoption of Medicare in July 1966 (the implementation date) acts as the catalyst for change (the key predictor variable to examine the effect).

Although there are four possible ways to analyze the intervention effect of Medicare and Medicaid on the percentage change in health care spending, only one of these is logical given the abrupt temporary nature of the data:

$$Y_t = (\omega_0/(1-\delta B)) * (1-B)I_t + N_t \qquad (3.1)$$

The dependent variable (Y_t) in this system represents increases in federal health care spending, and the model itself is designed to examine whether Medicare had a significant impact on this. In many ways, this can be viewed as an original confirmatory model to support the argument that Medicare significantly changed the structure of federal spending on health care. The results show that, as expected, there was indeed a significant impact from the establishment of Medicare on federal health care spending in 1966 and 1967.

The AR (1) parameter is significant and less than one. Recall that the AR (1) parameter indicates that there is an effect from the previous events (in this case spending) on the present. Likewise, the δ parameter indicates that the rate at which the effect of the intervention dissipates is significant, which means that there was an eventual decline in federal health care spending increases. This shows that federal health care spending eventually resumed to the path dependent nature it had followed before 1966. That is not to say that spending returned to pre-Medicare levels, rather that spending increases returned rapidly to pre-Medicare levels. Finally, the Q statistic of 15 confirms that the residuals are, in fact, white noise—that is, they are due to random elements and nothing more—and the model has captured the process ($\chi^2 = 15.51$ with 8 degrees of freedom at the 0.05 level). However, this effect should have been temporary, thus, the ω_0 parameter, which represents the abrupt and temporary intervention of Medicare, is significant and positive indicating that the path dependent system was, in fact, disrupted and propelled upward by Medicare.

Time Series Regression

Although time series data is unique and is generally not amenable to the same statistical analyses as non-time series data, it is possible to estimate regression models using times series data. This requires the use of any of a number of specialized regression techniques that compensate for the autocorrelation. These are widely available in any statistical package. In this case, I used a lagged regression model (Ostrom, 1990) to examine whether public mood affects public spending on health care. The analyses presented in chapter 3 show how public opinion on health care translates into public policy on health care.

In chapter 3, I used the Cochrane–Orcutt lagged regression model (Ostrom, 1990) to estimate the following model:

$$\text{Federal Health Care Spending}_t = \text{Health Policy Mood}_t + \text{Federal Health Care Spending}_{t-1} + N_t \qquad (3.2)$$

First, the residuals are, in fact, white noise and, thus, as discussed earlier, provide no confounding effect, and the Durbin–Watson Statistic of 1.25 suggests that there is no positive autocorrelation, thus the model controls the autocorrelation problem. As I explained in chapter 3, the results of this model show that the public mood does indeed have an impact on federal health care spending, even in the presence of strong controls for the path dependent budgeting process.

Forecasting

One of the alluring features of a time series model is the ability to predict the future. That is to say that by using a time series model, like the one in equation 3.2, it is possible to predict the future of the series through a technique known as "forecasting." The results of the model were used to forecast the percentage of federal spending on health care for the period 1960–1994. The data used are yearly health expenditure data collected by the Congressional Budget Office and Stimson's (1999) public mood on health care. Using this simple model to forecast future federal spending on health care, I find that, overall, the model was able to predict federal spending on health care quite well (see Figure 3.3). The residual mean square error of 2.89 gives a relative margin of error for the predictions, and as Figure 3.3 shows, the overall error is small. Generally, time series data can yield a wealth of information about a process when the appropriate methods are used.

CHAPTER 4 METHODS

Chapter 4 also relies on time series, however, in this situation, the series is based on a pooled collection of data at various time points. That is to say that it is a series of observations that cut across space and time. In chapter 4, the framework of the data is based in presidential advocacy. Thus, measures of policy proposals and passage are used as the skeleton upon which the data set was assembled. The measures of policy proposal and passage (which I will describe more fully) were then matched on a quarterly basis with data from multiple sources of individual series variables: Presidential Liberalism, Advocacy, Health Policy Attitude, Proposal, Presidential Popularity, Divided Government, Approval, and Climate.

Unique Problems with Chapter Four Data

IDENTIFICATION
The system of equations presented in chapter 4:

Proposed $= \beta_0 + \beta_1$ House Liberalism $+ \beta_2$ Senate Liberalism $+$
β_3 Presidential Liberalism $+ \beta_4$ Mandate $+$
β_5 Advocacy $+ \beta_6$ Health Policy Attitude $+ \epsilon$ (4.1)

Policy Approved $= \beta_0 + \beta_1$ Presidential Popularity $+$
β_2 Senate Liberalism $+ \beta_3$ House Liberalism $+$
β_4 Mandate $+ \beta_5$ Climate $+$
β_6 Divided Government $+ \beta_7$ Hazard Rate $+$
β_8 Residuals $+ \epsilon$ (4.2)

establishes a selection model using Presidential Liberalism; Advocacy and Health Policy Attitudes uniquely predict Proposal; and Presidential Popularity, Divided Government, and Climate uniquely predict approval of the presidential policy. One challenge in constructing a two-stage model is that the equations themselves must be identified; that is to say, the values of the equations must be determinable outside of the equation. For this to be true, there must be more excluded exogenous variables in a given equation than there are included endogenous variables. The outcome equation is identified when the order condition is met: $K_e > M_i - 1$, where K_e is the number of excluded exogenous variables and M_i is the number of included endogenous variables. In equation 4.2, there are two included endogenous variables (Policy Approved and the Hazard Rate) and three excluded exogenous variables (Presidential Liberalism, Advocacy, and Health Policy Attitude) yielding $3 > 2 - 1$, thus equation 4.2 meets the order condition.

MONTHLY, QUARTERLY, OR ANNUAL DATA?
As noted earlier, the data set was constructed with advocacy in mind. As a result, the data set used in the analysis is based on quarterly measures of presidential popularity and public mood between 1953 (the start of President Eisenhower's

first term) and 1996 (the end of President Clinton's first term) producing a total of 172 observations. Upon examination of the data, one may question the use of quarterly measures, given that monthly data is available for presidential popularity and for both dependent variables. In building the research design and establishing the data collection parameters, it is necessary to determine the ideal unit of analysis. Within this calculation, it is important to consider the efficiency of the data collection effort versus the information that is needed to properly estimate models. While quarterly measures do indeed reduce the information in the model, they provide a reasonable compromise, given that most of the other variables are annual. Although it is possible to use either yearly measures for all or monthly measures, each has its own associated problems. Annual measures ignore much of the changing nature of data observed on presidential popularity and policy proposals, thereby providing less explanatory power for the model. Using monthly data, while providing more information on the three variables observable at this level, does little more than increase the sample size.

AUTOCORRELATION

Time series data usually raises concern over the possibility of autocorrelation. The model illustrated in equations 4.1 and 4.2 addresses any problems of autocorrelation through the estimation technique itself. However, the problem of autocorrelation in the first-stage equation (4.1) remains as a possibility. A Durbin–Watson test fails to settle this in that it yields a d-statistic of 1.595, which, with 172 cases and six explanatory variables, places this model in the "zone of indecision." One solution to compensate for autocorrelation is to use an estimation technique other than ordinary least squares, where autocorrelation violates a crucial assumption for the production of BLUE (Best Linear Unbiased Estimates) parameter estimates. Indeed, in this case, the model is estimated using probabilistic regression (Probit). Given that Probit is a maximum likelihood technique designed to compensate for heteroscedastic errors, there should be little danger posed from the potential autocorrelation problem in the selection estimation.

This first-stage equation is also estimated using a robust standard errors routine in STATA 6.0, the results of which are reported in Table A.1. This table presents the results of the estimation of the selection equation using a robust standard errors routine to control for the probability of autocorrelation. In comparing this table with Table 4.2, the reader will see that even in the presence of robust standard errors, the significance levels do not change.

WHAT TO DO WHEN THE DEPENDENT VARIABLE IN THE OUTCOME
EQUATION IS DICHOTOMOUS

Generally speaking, when we use two-stage modeling techniques, whether in a selection equation system like the one presented here or in a nonrecursive equation like the one presented in chapter 5, we assume that the distributions

TABLE A.1

Selection Equation (proposed as dependent) with Robust Standard Errors ($N = 172$)

	β	SE
House Liberalism	−0.42***	0.114
Senate Liberalism	0.29***	0.110
Presidential Liberalism	0.31***	0.087
Mandate	0.29	0.410
Advocacy	0.01	0.045
Health Policy Attitude	3.11***	1.187
Constant	−3.31**	1.076
Log Likelihood = −86.646		
Chi^2 = 36.01		

**$p < .05$. ***$p < .001$

for both dependent variables are normally distributed (thereby having all of the desirable properties of a normal distribution) and that the dependent variable in the outcome equation is continuous. When the outcome equation is not continuous, we need to handle the situation in a different manner, while still meeting the underlying assumption of normality so that the distributions of our selection variable and our outcome variable match (in other words, we cannot compare apples and oranges). The solution in this case is using a two-stage model in which both stages are estimated using a probit technique because Probit assumes an underlying normal distribution for a dichotomous variable. In terms of the actual estimation procedure, the mechanics are quite straightforward. Equation 4.1 predicts the likelihood that the president will make a proposal and relies on variables that are likely suspects to explain that event. Equation 4.2 takes the censoring into account (i.e., a policy not proposed cannot be passed) in order to model the likelihood of a presidential policy initiative succeeding. If the dependent variable in the outcome equation is continuous, then one could model this using Tobit (see Breen, 1996; Greene, 1997; Long, 1997). However, the dichotomous nature of the dependent variable in the outcome equation requires a different method of modeling this system of equations.

The problem with the Tobit approach for this system is that the assumption is that the variance of the error in regard to the independent variables is equal to one. This is not so when both the selection and the outcome equation have a dichotomous dependent variable. This assumption is critical for accurate calculations of the standard errors for the regression coefficient and the calculation of the variance of the predicted value of the dependent variable. Violating this assumption affects the calculation of the standard errors, generally attenuating them. While Probit normally corrects for heteroscedasticity, it is less successful when used in a two-stage process. Because of this, Rivers and Vuong (1988) recommend a two-stage modeling technique that is generally superior. This is because the residuals from the selection equation are modeled as an independent variable, serving to "soak up" the correlation between the disturbances in the two equations. Further, they provide a built-in test for success in that a nonsignificant coefficient for the disturbances in the second equation indicates that the cross-correlation between equations is controlled.

Hence, I proceeded with the 2SCML (two-stage conditional maximum likelihood) system of equations outlined earlier. The first equation was estimated using Probit and a hazard rate was calculated. The residuals from the equation were then saved for incorporation as independent variables in the outcome equation. The hazard rate controls for the selection process and the inclusion of the residuals provides a means of controlling for the correlation of the disturbances across equations normally associated with two-stage estimation techniques. Additionally, in that this data is essentially a time series, the inclusion of the errors serves as a correction for the potential of autocorrelation. In fact, this technique is similar to the time series technique "error correction mechanism" wherein the inclusion of the error term as a variable controls for the correlation of the errors across point-in-time observations (Greene 1997; Hamilton, 1994, pp. 580–581). Finally, the estimation itself provides a test for the success of this method in purging the correlations of the disturbances; indeed, the nonsignificant coefficient for the error term suggests a successful correction (Rivers & Vuong, 1988).

Description of the Variables in Chapter Four

DEPENDENT VARIABLES

Proposed is a dichotomous variable coded as one if, in a given quarter, the president proposed a liberal health policy initiative designed to extend or expand the role of the federal government in health care and zero otherwise. To define this variable Peterson's (1990) criteria for president policy proposals is used. First, the proposal must be innovative to some degree, it must seek to change the status quo, and it must have been presented in some manner, by the president, to demonstrate that it is a request for legislation. The reader will note that with few exceptions these are policies that were also identified by Mayhew (1991) and Cameron (2000). The primary source for this data was *The Public Papers of the Presidents of the United States: 1932 to 1994*. Presidents were also allowed multiple proposals, although only one such proposal was recorded per quarter.

Policy Approved is a dichotomous variable coded as one if Congress approved the president's proposal for extending federal involvement in health care and zero otherwise. The primary source for this data is the *Congressional Quarterly Almanac*. Only those actions correlated with presidential requests are included. Further, as Table 4.1 shows, policy proposals were not allowed to carry over from president to president. Thus, although President Kennedy advocated for Medicare, it is President Johnson who gets credit for the passage.

INDEPENDENT VARIABLES

With the exception of Advocacy, all of the independent variables were rescaled on a zero to one scale.

House Liberalism is taken from Stimson, MacKuen, and Erikson (1995). The measure was created by averaging liberalism scores reported by interest groups (Americans for Democratic Action [ADA], American Conservative Association [ACA], American Conservative Union [ACU]) for the members of the House of Representatives. This variable is included in the selection equation as a measure of the receptiveness of the members of the House to the liberal policy change proposed by the president. Further, this variable is included as a proxy for partisanship, in that party identification would seem to be a better predictor of policy approval, given the tendency of the members of Congress to vote as a block with their president.

Senate Liberalism is taken from Stimson et al. (1995). The measure was created by averaging liberalism scores reported by interest groups (ADA, ACA/ACU) for the members of the Senate. This variable is included in the selection equation as a measure of the receptiveness of the members of the Senate to the liberal policy change proposed by the president. Further, this variable is included as a proxy for partisanship, in that party identification would seem to be a better predictor of policy approval, given the tendency of the members of Congress to vote as a block with their president.

Presidential Liberalism, as calculated by Stimson et al. (1995) is the mean ADA score of the policy support group in the Congress for the president. It is included primarily as a control on the theory that more liberal presidents will be more likely to propose liberal policy changes.

Mandate is a measure of the effect of a president's electoral college victory. The margin of victory in the electoral college is commonly used as an indicator of whether the president has achieved a "landslide" victory. Further, in Conley's (2001) models, electoral votes are consistently the best predictor of presidential mandate claims. However, the research also shows that the impact of electoral college victories dissipates. As a result, this variable was given a six-month half-life on the theory that the effect of a mandate dissipates rather quickly. Thus, an initial mandate of 80% is reduced to 40% at the start of the third quarter of the first year in office, and 20% at the start of the president's second year, and 10% by the time midterm elections come about. I should note that the average of the first year Mandate scores that I calculate and use in this model correlate with Conley's "First Year Presidential Success Scores (p. 74) at 0.68. Thus, as a component of context and a predictor of presidential success, this variable is well grounded in existing studies.

Advocacy is a simple tally measure of the total number of advocacy groups opposed to national health care legislation subtracted from the total number of groups in favor. For example, a program like Medicare was discussed early in the Kennedy administration, however, at that time, the advocacy groups like the National Council on Aging and the American Association of Retired Persons were in their formative stages and, thus, were not active in the effort. Conversely, the American Medical Association and the National Insurance Association of America were active against any federal provision of health care dating back to the Truman administration. By 1964, this balance shifted as more elderly and children's advocacy groups joined to encourage a federal role in the provision of health care to these groups.

Health Policy Attitude is a measure created to model how receptive the public is to an expanded role of government in health care. This variable was created by multiplying Stimson's (1999) health policy mood (whether people want more government involvement in health care) by his size of government mood score and dividing the resulting number by 100 to return it to the mood scale range.

Presidential Popularity is a quarterly average of favorable responses to the Gallup Opinion Poll question "Do you approve or disapprove of the way .(president's name) is handling his job as president?"

Climate is Stimson's (1999) public mood score rescaled between zero and one. This is a measure of public attitudes toward the size of government and is thus a good measure of the willingness of the public to accept or reject an expansion of governmental action in a policy area.

Divided Government is a quarterly measure based on Mayhew's (1991) coding of this phenomenon. In this case, the variable is dichotomous, coded as one when at least one house of the legislature is in opposition to the president and zero otherwise.

CHAPTER 5 METHODS

Unlike the data used in chapters 3 and 4, the data used in chapter 5 is not a time series, thus the special situations that existed for handling time series data are not a problem in chapter 5. Nevertheless, the data in chapter 5 are complicated by a series of different technical problems associated with the nature of the data. These include endogeneity, a situation where values for a variable are determined within a system rather than externally, as is normally the case. Further, as mentioned in the discussion of the data in chapter 4, the data in chapter 5 are complicated by the fact that in the models used the outcome equation is dichotomous, necessitating a specialized approach to the normal cure for endogeneity, the use of a two-stage model.

Problems of Estimations with Endogeneity

As noted, the data used in chapter 5 presents unique concerns. Because of the problems of estimation caused by the correlation of the dependent variable with the error terms, and also the correlation between the estimated error terms for each equation, it is necessary to create estimates of the two reciprocal causation variables Support and Knowledge that are uncorrelated with the error terms. For example, in the Knowledge equation estimated in chapter 5, there is some correlation between the estimate of *Knowledge* and the estimated error (ϵ) for that equation. Using the estimate of Knowledge in the Support equation will bias the results because of the correlation between the error term now included in the estimate of Knowledge. Using the predicted Knowledge values as predictors of support causes the error term of the Knowledge equation (A.1) to become correlated with the estimate for *Support* (equation A.2) that are excluded from the estimation. This produces biased coefficient estimates. Working through the following substitutions can show this:

$$\text{Support} = \beta_0 + \beta_1 \text{ Knowledge} + \beta_2 \text{ Democrat} + \beta_3 \text{ Republican} +$$
$$\beta_4 \text{ Clinton} + \beta_5 \text{ Bush} + \beta_6 \text{ Education} + \beta_7 \text{ Income} + \epsilon \quad (A.2)$$

$$\text{Knowledge} = \beta_0 + \beta_1 \text{ Support} + \beta_2 \text{ Income} + \beta_3 \text{ Education} + \epsilon \quad (A.1)$$

Substituting equation A.1 for *Knowledge* in equation A.2 yields equation A.3:

$$\text{Support} = \beta_0 + \beta_1 (\beta_0 + \beta_1 \text{ Support} + \beta_2 \text{ Income} +$$
$$\beta_3 \text{ Education} + \epsilon) + \beta_2 \text{ Democrat} + \beta_3 \text{ Republican} +$$
$$\beta_4 \text{ Clinton} + \beta_5 \text{ Bush} + \beta_6 \text{ Education} + \beta_7 \text{ Income} + \epsilon \quad (A.3)$$

Looking at equation A.3, it is evident that the predicted value of *Support* in equation A.2 using the estimated value for *Knowledge* from equation A.1 is correlated with the error term from equation A.1.

If this were to be left uncorrected, the effects of the variables would be muted because they would not be clean measures of support or policy given the fact that the two are determinants of each other. That is to say that in a system where knowledge and support are defined by each other, it is impossible to know what the true effect of knowledge is on support. Thus, it is necessary to estimate new measures that can be used in place of these variables so that the true effect of knowledge on support can be discovered. This is accomplished by employing variables that can legitimately be excluded from the estimation without any effect on the dependent variable.[1] These are referred to as "instrumental variables" and if the model is well thought out and based in sound theory, they should be neither substantively nor statistically significant in predicting the variable to be estimated. These models are estimated in a system of reduced-form equations where the endogenous variables are purged of the correlations with the error term because the reciprocal causation variables are excluded from the estimation, yielding generally unbiased coefficient estimates. The reduced-form equations are:

$$\text{Knowledge} = \pi_1 \text{ Income} + \pi_2 \text{ Education} + \pi_3 \text{ Democrat} +$$
$$\pi_4 \text{ Republican} + \pi_5 \text{ Clinton} + \pi_6 \text{ Bush} + v_1 \qquad \text{(A.4)}$$

and,

$$\text{Support} = \pi_7 \text{ Income} + \pi_8 \text{ Education} + \pi_9 \text{ Democrat} +$$
$$\pi_{10} \text{ Republican} + \pi_{11} \text{ Clinton} + \pi_{12} \text{ Bush} + v_2 \qquad \text{(A.5)}$$

If the process is properly modeled, as per the literature on political knowledge, the expectation is that *Income* and *Education* will be the only significant variables in the estimation of equation A.4 and that each will be positively signed. Conversely, the expectation for the results of equation A.5, *Income* and *Education* will be neither substantively nor statistically significant. Further there is an expectation, driven by theory, that the signaling variables (*Clinton* and *Bush*) and the cuing variables (*Democrat* and *Republican*) may be significant predictors of *Support* in equation A.5.

Traditionally, linear probability models were used. While these estimation techniques capture the essence of the relationship, they are not accurate because they assume a linear relationship that does not exist for more than 40% of the range of the dependent variable. Thus, to estimate the model properly, a maximum likelihood estimation technique is required. One possibility is the Two-Stage-Probit-Least-Squares technique discussed in Alvarez (1994). But, as Alvarez notes, "Monte Carlo simulations demonstrate that the standard errors are generally too small" (p. 8). Traditionally for problems like this, researchers have relied on correction procedures such as Heckman's correction. The problem with this technique is that there is an assumption that one can know the value of Ω (the weighting matrix) for the standard errors (in ordinary least squares this is assumed to be unity). However, determining the true value of Ω in a situation with a heteroscedastic error term is not possible. Thus, a method for estimation, such as 2SCML, that accounts for the true nature of the errors is better.

TABLE A.2

Reduced Form Results: Knowledge as Dependent Variable ($N = 680$)

	β	SE
Cuing Variables		
Democrat	.017	.023
Republican	−.024	.025
Clinton	.039	.026
Bush	−.041	.026
Socioeconomic Variables		
Income	.036***	.012
Education	.049***	.015
Constant	−.237***	.034
$R^2 = .08$		
adj $R^2 = .07$		

***$p < .001$

In terms of the estimation procedure, the first stage of the 2SCML process is similar to the linear probability model in that the reduced form equations must be estimated to produce estimates of the endogenous variables that are uncorrelated with the error terms. These estimates are presented in Tables A.2 and A.3.

The 2SCML is straightforward, although the reader is advised to consult Alvarez (1994) and Rivers and Vuong (1988) for an in-depth discussion. To briefly summarize the procedure, the reduced form equations estimations are performed for the ordinary least squares model and the predicted values and residuals are saved. The second stage is a probit in which the saved residuals from the ordinary least squares model are used as a predictor variable. This also provides a built-in test for exogeneity, if the estimate for the residuals is non-significant as a predictor, it is an indication that the endogenous variable has been made exogenous.

Table A.2 shows the results of the reduced form equation estimates for the Knowledge model. The two instrumental variables in this equation, Education and Income have statistically significant ($p < .002$) effects. Further, across the range of these variables, the effects are substantively significant. For example, with Education, moving from high school education or less to graduate or professional education, produces on average a 10% increase in the Knowledge scale of zero to one holding all other variables constant. The effect

TABLE A.3
Reduced Form Results: Support as Dependent Variable ($N = 680$)

	β	SE
Cuing Variables		
Democrat	.263**	.139
Republican	−.032	.149
Clinton	.739***	.147
Bush	−.734***	.151
Socioeconomic Variables		
Income	.119	.090
Education	−.021	.071
Constant	−.329*	.202
Log Likelihood = −344.888		
Percent Correctly Predicted = 73.48		
Reduction in Error = 48.4%		

*$p < .10$. **$p < .05$. ***$p < .001$

for Income is substantively significant as well in that moving from poor to wealthy raises the predicted Knowledge score by 11% on average, holding all other variables constant. The effect here is only important in relation to how they perform in the Support equation from which they are excluded. If the system is correctly specified, they should be nonsignificant.

Table A.3 shows that the instrumental variables Clinton and Bush attain statistical significance ($p < .0001$) while the control variables Republican and Democrat are split ($p < .828$ and $P < .058$, respectively). Democrat has the expected positive sign and a large coefficient. When transformed to a probability, on average, identifying as a Democrat increases the average probability of supporting the Health Security Act by 59%, holding all other variables at zero. Both Republican and Democrat are, as noted, statistically nonsignificant in the Knowledge model.

Description of the Variables in Chapter 5

DEPENDENT VARIABLE

Support is coded as one if the respondent indicated that he or she approved of the Health Security Act strongly or somewhat, and zero otherwise.

INDEPENDENT VARIABLES

Democrat is coded as one if the respondent identified as a Democrat and zero otherwise.

Clinton is coded as one if the respondent indicated voting for Clinton in 1992 and zero otherwise.

Knowledge is taken from a series of five questions regarding respondent knowledge about the Health Security Act. Each correct response was coded as a one and each incorrect response was coded as a zero. The scores were summed for each respondent and then divided by five. This variable ranges from 0 to 1 and is discrete along intervals of 0.20. The modal response was two correct.

Income is coded as zero (poor) if the respondent indicated income below $12,000, one (lower middle class) if the respondent indicated income greater than $12,000 but less than $30,000, two (upper middle class) if the respondent indicated income of greater than $30,000 but less than $75,000, and three (wealthy) if the respondent indicated income greater than $75,000.

Education is coded as one if the respondent indicated education of high school or less, two if the respondent indicated some college or college graduate, and three if the respondent indicated graduate or professional education.

CHAPTER SIX METHODS

Due to the limitations of these data, a single-stage probit model was employed, relying on the quasi-experimental design (Achen, 1986) to purify the Ad Exposure variable of its correlations with the party and elite variables.[2] One would expect to observe similar results to the previous model for the party and elite variables, with Clinton and Democrat emerging as positive predictors of support and Dole (the new conservative elite)[3] and Republican emerging as negative predictors of support. Likewise, one would expect the variable measuring the effect of the countervalent message to have a significant negative effect. This study relied on a quasi-experimental (see Achen, 1986) use of survey data. The benefit of using survey data is, of course, that it relies on a random sample of the population of the United States and as a result has a high external validity and generalizability. The disadvantage is that even in a quasi-experimental data set, there is a loss of internal validity. That is to say, there is a possibility of confounding effects, although the data were collected using statistically valid sampling techniques and state-of-the-art survey design. As Neuman, Just, and Crigler (1992) suggest, one way to confirm and add greater understanding to the results obtained in the high external validity setting of a survey is to explore the same issues in an experimental design where internal validity is increased, albeit at the expense of external validity. Indeed, in the experimental setting, internal validity is increased because exposure to the media is controlled and randomly assigned, whereas in the survey setting exposure relies on recall and self-selection, although the sample is designed to represent the general population. Neuman et al. argue that for these very reasons using the two methods together provides much greater understanding and confidence in the findings than either could alone.

Description of the Variables in Chapter 6

DEPENDENT VARIABLES

Support is coded as one if the respondent indicated that he or she approved of the Health Security Act strongly or somewhat, and zero otherwise.

Change is coded as one if the participant changed their health policy preference to Health Care as a public/private partnership from some other metaphor following the priming.

INDEPENDENT VARIABLES

Democrat is coded as one if the respondent identified as a Democrat and zero otherwise.

Clinton is coded as one if the respondent indicated the intention of voting for Clinton in 1996 and zero otherwise.

Dole is coded as one if the respondent indicated the intention of voting for Dole in 1996 and zero otherwise.

Ad Exposure is coded as one if the respondent reported seeing the "Harry and Louise" advertisement and zero otherwise.

Income is coded as zero (poor) if the respondent indicated income below $12,000, one (lower middle class) if the respondent indicated income greater than $12,000 but less than $30,000, two (upper middle class) if the respondent indicated income of greater than $30,000 but less than $75,000, and three (wealthy) if the respondent indicated income greater than $75,000.

Education is coded as one if the respondent indicated education of high school or less, two if the respondent indicated some college or college graduate, and three if the respondent indicated graduate or professional education.

Treatment is coded as one if the participant was in one of the three (Clinton/Gore/Bradley) conditions and zero if the participant was in the control group.

Political Sophistication is the percentage of correct responses to the Delli-Carpini and Keeter (1996) scale of political sophistication recoded between zero (no correct answers) and one (all questions answered correctly).

Health Care Sophistication is the percentage of correct responses to the Chard (2002) and Schlesinger and Lau (2000) scale of health policy sophistication recoded between zero (no correct answers) and one (all questions answered correctly).

Ideology is coded from zero (conservative) to one (liberal) on a five-point scale.

CHAPTER 7 METHODS

The study presented in chapter 7, like the study in chapter 6, relied on a quasi-experimental (see Achen, 1986) use of survey data. Likewise, in Chapter 6, I discussed the virtues of using survey data: It relies on a random sample of the population of the United States; it has a high external validity; and, it is generalizeable. The disadvantages (even in a quasi-experimental data set) include a loss of internal validity, a possibility of confounding effects, a reliance on recall, and self-selection. As discussed in chapter 6, Neuman et al. (1992) suggest that using an experimental design provides one way to confirm and add greater understanding to the results obtained in a survey. Although, an experiment is not random and is not representative of the general public, it has higher internal validity because exposure to the media is controlled and randomly assigned.

Description of the Variables in Chapter 7

DEPENDENT VARIABLES

Clinton is coded as one if the respondent indicated intention to vote for Clinton in 1996 and zero otherwise.

FTBradley is Standard National Election Study Feeling-Thermometer question regarding Bill Bradley where 0 is cold and 100 is hot.

FTGore is Standard National Election Study Feeling-Thermometer question regarding Al Gore where 0 is cold and 100 is hot.

INDEPENDENT VARIABLES

Exposure is coded as one if the respondent reported seeing the "Harry and Louise" advertisement and zero otherwise.

Support is coded as one if the respondent indicated that he or she approved of the Health Security Act strongly or somewhat, and zero otherwise.

*Interaction (Exposure * Support)* is a multiplicative interaction term created by multiplying the variables *Exposure* and *Support*.

Democrat is coded as one if the respondent identified as a Democrat and zero otherwise.

Republican is coded as one if the respondent identified as a Republican and zero otherwise.

Income is dollars in thousands coded as a mean dollar amount for the income range indicated by the respondent.

Education is coded as one if the respondent indicated education of high school or less, two if the respondent indicated some college or college graduate, and three if the respondent indicated graduate or professional education.

Media Exposure is coded as one if the respondent was randomly assigned to the treatment group (health care story) and zero otherwise (filler stories only).

HealthCare is coded as zero for conservative attitudes on health care and one for liberal attitudes on health care.

Interaction (Exposure * Support) is a multiplicative term created by multiplying the variables *MediaExposure* and *HealthCare*.

Ideology is self-reported ideology on a scale from one (liberal) to five (conservative).

EXPERIMENTAL QUESTIONS AND TREATMENTS IN CHAPTERS 6 AND 7

Domain-Specific Policy Questions

1. Please indicate your level of agreement with this statement: In the United States, health care costs are rising faster than the cost of living.

Strongly Disagree	Disagree	No Opinion	Agree	Strongly Agree
1	2	3	4	5

2. Please indicate your level of agreement with this statement: Medicare is a government program providing health care coverage for the elderly.

Strongly Disagree	Disagree	No Opinion	Agree	Strongly Agree
1	2	3	4	5

3. Please indicate your level of agreement with this statement: The United States spends more on health care than any other country.

Strongly Disagree	Disagree	No Opinion	Agree	Strongly Agree
1	2	3	4	5

4. Please indicate your level of agreement with this statement: Most uninsured families have at least one member employed.

Strongly Disagree	Disagree	No Opinion	Agree	Strongly Agree
1	2	3	4	5

5. If you had to pick one of the following as the percentage of the federal budget dedicated to health care spending, which do you think would come the closest?

25%	33%	50%	75%
1	2	3	4

6. Taking all of the money spent by people in the United States for things like cars and houses and other goods and services people can buy, what percentage do you think comes closest to the amount spent on health care?

15%	30%	45%	60%
1	2	3	4

7. Please indicate your level of agreement with this statement: Medicaid is a program providing health insurance to the elderly.

Strongly Disagree	Disagree	No Opinion	Agree	Strongly Agree
1	2	3	4	5

Sample Treatment Article

WASHINGTON (AP) Today President Bill Clinton unveiled his new health care plan to expand health care coverage for those who do not have it and improve it for those who do. The focus of the new plan is to expand access to affordable health insurance for every child by 2005 and make health coverage more affordable for millions of adults. Clinton plans to draw on the private employer based health insurance system in the United States and expand the public health insurance plans Medicare and Medicaid to ensure that all Americans have access to affordable health care by 2005.

As Clinton detailed this plan, he outlined five steps that he states will improve every aspect of the health care system. They are: (1) assuring rights for patients by passing legislation to keep medical records private and a strong enforceable Patients' Bill of Rights that gives patients critical protections, such as access to specialists, access to emergency room services and making health plans accountable for harming patients; (2) modernizing health care by focusing on prevention, individual responsibility, and new technologies to improve and measure quality; (3) building on the progress and possibilities of new research while protecting against the perils, such as genetic discrimination; (4) addressing the nations' unprecedented challenges due to the aging of the baby boomers by strengthening and modernizing Medicare, including providing a prescription drug benefit, and by proposing initiatives to support families with long-term care needs; and (5) working toward the goal of assuring all Americans have access to quality health care coverage.

Clinton's plan consists of major initiatives that he claims are designed to deal with the problem of uninsured Americans and high health care costs. Specifically, Clinton wants to ensure that all children have access to affordable health insurance by 2005. Clinton's second stated goal is to expand Health Care Coverage for Working

Parents who cannot afford or are not eligible for health insurance. Clinton's third goal is to provide affordable health care options for Americans between the ages of 55 and 65, the fastest growing group of uninsured in the country, with more than 3 million currently without health insurance, over 60 percent of whom are women. Clinton's fourth goal is to guarantee people with disabilities and pre-existing conditions access to health care if they return to work. Under current law, people with disabilities are often forced to drop health care coverage because they get a job that makes them ineligible for Medicaid or Medicare because of their income or ability to work. Finally, Clinton wants to strengthen community health centers, public hospitals, academic medical centers, and other safety net providers that treat millions of Americans. Clinton intends to use these public facilities to augment public health insurance coverage for the uninsured.

Clinton plans to accomplish his goals by expanding the public health insurance programs, Medicare and Medicaid to new groups not currently eligible and by strengthening the existing private employer based insurance and health care delivery system through tax incentives and regulation.

Notes

CHAPTER 1

1. Medicare is a federal program funded through a payroll deduction on the current workforce and premiums from enrollees to provide comprehensive health care insurance to the elderly and disabled. Its counterpart, Medicaid, is a joint program between the states and the federal government, funded through tax revenues, to provide health care for indigents and children. Increasingly, Medicaid is being used by the elderly to finance the costs of long-term care.

CHAPTER 3

1. Much of the historical discussion of social constructions is necessarily based on extrapolation and inference because of the lack of empirical data. I have therefore relied on statements by and about groups to estimate reasonable social constructions for the target populations.

2. Schneider and Ingram then make the argument that each of these categories represents a level of support for public policy as well as the allocation of benefits and burdens. For example, a topic that has received much attention is welfare. There is no argument that recipients of welfare by and large fit into the dependent category. According to Schneider and Ingram, groups in this category will have undersubscribed benefits and oversubscribed burdens. In simpler terms, this means that dependents will not receive the benefits they need, but will be accused of receiving more benefits than they deserve. Thus, welfare reform becomes a major policy issue because of the target group's social construction. In contrast, we hear little about curtailing veterans' pensions because veterans are in the advantaged category, wherein benefits are oversubscribed and burdens are undersubscribed.

3. The contemporaneous impact C_0 is simply b_1 ($C_0 = b_1$).

CHAPTER 4

1. A complete list of variables used in the models along with coding explanations appears in the Methodological Appendix. However, in this section and the following sections, the variables that appear in the model (see equations 4.1 and 4.2 in the "Data and Method" section later in this chapter) are listed parenthetically in *bold* following the passage in which they are first mentioned in theory and thereafter will be capitalized.

2. Other domestic issues, such as education and criminal justice, have similar qualities; however, until recently, these policy areas have been primarily the provinces of the states. One area that would be interesting to examine using the analysis presented in this manuscript is federal trade policy. Like health care, trade policy has the dual properties of being important economically and usually highly salient.

3. Thus, one could say the public indirectly shapes policy by placing constraints on the president and Congress. Members of Congress are constrained by their focus on constituency service (Kingdon, 1989) while the president's influence is constrained through popularity. Further, the public, through interest groups can destabilize the policy arena (Baumgartner & Jones, 1993; McCarthy, McPhail, & Smith, 1996; Roberts & King, 1996).

4. A community rating system is simply one in which each contributor pays the same share of the overall payments made by the plan. Thus, someone who was hospitalized for four months would pay the same premium as someone who had not been to the doctor in two years.

5. This ignores legislative initiatives that need not be proposed by the president in that they are beyond the scope of this research.

CHAPTER 5

1. All data and documentation to replicate this analysis are available from ICPSR (#6287). I thank the Inter-University Consortium for Political and Social Research for providing me with *The Washington Post "Health Care Poll of October 1993."* The data were originally collected by Chilton Research for *The Washington Post.* Neither ICPSR nor the original collectors of the data bear any responsibility for the analyses or interpretation presented here. All statistical analyses contained in this study were performed using Stata for Windows.

2. The percentages in the election were as follows: 43.2% for Clinton, 37.7% for Bush, and 19.0% for Perot. The Bush vote is the most discrepant, with a difference of 4.5%; Perot follows with a 1.8% difference; and the Clinton vote differs by only 0.03%.

3. In terms of education and income, the respondents were diverse, with 10.7% (80) respondents indicating graduate or professional education while the remaining respondents split between high school or less (40.7%) and college (48.5%). Likewise, income is well dispersed, with 9.3% categorized as poor (below the poverty level), 29.3%

categorized as lower middle class, 49.7% categorized as upper middle class, and 11.8% categorized as wealthy.

4. The difference between a recursive system and a nonrecursive system comes from the error terms of the specified equations. In a recursive system, the error terms are assumed to be uncorrelated; thus, estimations can be made using the same independent variables and simply switching the variables exhibiting reciprocal causation from the independent variable side of the equation to the dependent variable side of the equation for each estimation. In a nonrecursive system, the error terms are assumed to be correlated; thus, to produce estimates of the variables exhibiting reciprocal causation, using instrumental variables whose values are determined completely outside the system is necessary. For interesting and recent uses of such models with policy implications see Alvarez and Nagler (1995) and Grier, Munger, and Roberts (1994).

5. This essentially removes the effect of partisanship by treating all people as if they were independents (the baseline category). This was done because the party identification variables Democrat and Republican proved to be nonsignificant.

6. When comparing standard probit results and 2SCML, the value of using the two-stage process can be seen by comparing the results of the standard probit model with the results of the two-stage model. In the two stage probit model, we see the "purified" effects of Knowledge. The purified Knowledge variable not only captures the indirect effects of education and income on support for the Health Security Act, but it also presents an unbiased estimate that is not correlated with the error term.

CHAPTER 6

1. Rather than using an interaction term to model this effect, the analysis of this second poll is more appropriate. First, interaction terms in a nonlinear model such as a single-equation probit are often difficult to interpret (see generally Greene, 1997). In my complex two-stage model, the interpretation of such effects would definitely cause the methodology to detract from the substance of this chapter. My use of a similar second poll addressing the Harry and Louise advertising campaign provides a better test of my model than the use of interaction terms.

2. I should note that Jacobs and Shapiro (2000) present a compelling argument that there is a reciprocal effect between media coverage and policy support; unfortunately, the data used in this model does not contain enough information to explore whether this relationship exists.

CHAPTER 7

1. Bradley stated that he would use the power of the presidency to push for universal health care. Additionally, he stated that he would use the federal surplus to extend health insurance to all Americans and to reduce childhood poverty: "I'd like to know

that every child in America has a chance to realize his or her potential. There are still 14 million children today who live in poverty. There are still 45 million people in America without health insurance" (Dao, 1999). Gore, on the other hand, favored incremental changes to existing policies and greater enforcement of existing legislation rather than the far-reaching reforms called for by Bradley.

2. The treatment group was further divided for another experiment that does not affect the present study.

3. Recall, my experiment was conducted from December 9, 1999, to January 21, 2000, concluding before the New Hampshire primary.

METHODOLOGICAL APPENDIX

1. All variables with the exception of *Advocacy* were rescaled on a zero to one scale.

2. For a general explanation of this process, see Berry (1984) and Gujarati (1995, 635–708). For more in-depth discussions, see Greene (1991: 578–634), Bartels (1991), and Hanushek and Jackson (1977).

3. I recognize the possibility that there may be some tendency of respondents to report their memory of exposure to the ad based partly on their feelings about the plan, but I believe that the controls in the multivariate model are likely to ameliorate this potential concern.

4. Senator Dole, as Senate minority leader and frontrunner for the 1996 Republican presidential nomination, had replaced George Bush as the dominant Republican elite by this time.

References

Aaron, H. J. (1991). *Serious and unstable condition: Financing America's health care.* Washington, DC: Brookings Institution.

Aaron, H. J. (1994, February 20). Cooper plan fatally flawed. *The Arizona Daily Star*, p. F-1.

Aaron, H. J., & Schwartz, W. B. (1984). *The painful prescription: Rationing hospital care.* Washington, DC: Brookings Institution.

Achen, C. H. (1986). *The statistical analysis of quasi-experiments.* Berkeley and Los Angeles: University of California Press.

Ainsworth, S. (1993). Regulating lobbyists and interest group influence. *Journal of Politics, 55*, 41–56.

Alchian, A. (1950). Uncertainty, evolution, and economic theory. *Journal of Political Economy, 58*, 211–221.

Aldrich, J. H., Sullivan, J. L. & Borgida, E. (1989). Foreign affairs and issue voting: Do presidential candidates "waltz before a blind audience?" *American Political Science Review, 83*(1), 123–141.

Allison, P. D. (1995). *Survival analysis using the SAS system.* Cary, NC: SAS Institute.

Alt, J. E., & Shepsle, K. (Eds.) (1994). *Perspectives on political economy.* New York: Cambridge University Press.

Althaus, S. (1996) Opinion polls, information effects and political equality: exploring ideological biases in collective opinion. *Political Communication, 13*, 3–21.

Althaus, S. (1998). Information effects in collective preferences. *American Political Sciance Review, 92*, 545–558.

Alvarez, R. M. (1994). *Two stage estimation of non-recursive choice models* (Social Science Working Paper 905). Pasadena: California Institute of Technology.

Anderson, O. (1989). *The health services continuum in democratic states.* Ann Arbor, MI: Health Administration Press.

Ansolabehere, S., & Iyengar, S. (1994). Riding the wave and claiming ownership over issues: The joint effects of advertising and news coverage in campaigns. *Public Opinion Quarterly, 58*(3), 335–357.

Ansolabehere, S., Iyengar, S., Simon, A., & Valentino, N. (1994). Does attack advertising demobilize the electorate? *American Political Science Review, 88*(4), 829–838.

Bartels, L. (1991). Instrumental and quasi instrumental variables. *American Journal of Political Science, 35,* 777–800.

Bartels, L. (1996). Uninformed votes: Information effects in presidential elections. *American Journal of Political Science, 40,* 194–230.

Baumgartner, F. R., & Jones, B. D. (1993). *Agendas and instability in American politics.* Chicago: University of Chicago Press.

Behr, R., & Iyengar, S. (1982). Television news, real-world cues, and changes in the public agenda. *Public Opinion Quarterly, 48,* 38–57.

Bennet, J. (1997, January 3). Clinton's New Year's Eve: Looking Back. *The New York Times,* p. A20.

Bennett, S. (1989). Trends in Americans' political information, 1967–87. *American Politics Quarterly, 17;* 422–485.

Berelson, B.R., Lazarsfeld, P. F., & McPhee, W. N. (1954). *Voting: A study of opinion formation in a presidential campaign.* Chicago: University of Chicago Press.

Berry, W. (1984) *Nonrecursive Causal Models.* Newbury Park, CA: Sage.

Blakenau, R. (1994). HCFA: Changing with the times. *Hospitals and Health Networks, 68,* 52–53.

Blumenthal, D. (1996). Effects of market reforms on doctors and their patients. *Health Affairs, 15,* 170–184.

Bond, J. R., & Fleisher, R. (1990). *The president in the legislative arena.* Chicago: University of Chicago Press.

Brace, P., & Hinckley, B. (1992). *Follow the leader.* New York: Basic Books.

Brace, P., & Hinckley, B. (1993). Presidential activities from Truman through Reagan: Timing and impact. *Journal of Politics, 55,* 382–398.

Brady, D. W., & Buckley, K. M. (1995). Health care reform in the 103rd Congress: A predictable failure. *Journal of Health Politics, Policy, and Law, 20,* 447–454.

Breen, R. (1996). *Regression models: Censored, sample selected, or truncated data.* Thousand Oaks, CA: Sage.

Brodie, M. (1996). Americans' political participation in the 1993–94 national health care reform debate. *Journal of Health Politics, Policy, and Law, 21,* 99–128

Brody, R., & Page, B. (1972). The assessment of policy voting. *American Political Science Review, 66,* 450–458.

Brody, R. A. (1984). International crises: A rallying point for the president. *Public Opinion, 6*, 41–60.

Brown, L. D. (1983). *Politics and health care organizations: HMOs as Federal Policy.* Washington, DC: Brookings Institution.

Brown, L. D. (1994). National health reform: An idea whose political time has come? *PS: Political Science and Politics, 27*, 198–201.

Burkhead, J. (1959). *Government budgeting.* New York: Wiley.

Calvert, R. (1985). The value of biased information: A rational choice model of political advice. *Journal of Politics, 47*, 530–555.

Calvert, R. L. (1987). Reputation and legislative leadership. *Public Choice, 55*, 81–121.

Cameron, C. M. (2000). *Veto bargaining: Presidents and the politics of negative power.* New York: Cambridge University Press.

Campbell, A. (1966). Surge and decline: A study of electoral change. In A. Campbell, P. E. Converse, W. Miller, & Donald Stokes (Eds)., *Elections and the Political Order* (Pp. 40–62). New York: Wiley.

Campbell, J. E. (1991). The presidential surge and its midterm decline in congressional elections, 1868–1988. *Journal of Politics, 53*, 477–487.

Carmines, E. G., & Stimson, J. A. (1986). On the structure and sequence of issue evolution. *American Political Science Review, 80*, 901–920.

Carter, S. (1997). *The feedback factor: Public opinion and the health care debate, 1993–94.* Paper presented at annual meeting of the Midwest Political Science Association, Chicago.

Chard, R. E. (2003). The state of health: Innovations in health policy. In R. Kinney & M. Harris (Eds.), *Entrepreneurs and innovation in state and local government* (pp. ____). New York: Lexington Books.

Chard, R. E., & Ling, C. (1999). Media priming of the Health Security Act: How Harry and Louise affected presidential vote intention. Paper presented at the annual meeting of the Midwest Political Science Association, Chicago.

Cobb, M., & Kuklinski, J. (1997). Changing minds: Political arguments and political persuasion. *American Journal of Political Science, 41*, 88–121.

Cobb, R. W., & Elder, C. W. (1983). *Participation in American politics: The dynamics of agenda-building.* Boston: Allyn & Bacon.

Cohen, J. E. (1995). Presidential rhetoric and the public agenda. *American Journal of Political Science, 39*, 87–107.

Coleman, V. (1985). *The story of medicine.* London: Robert Hale.

Congressional Budget Office. (1990). *Physician payment reform under medicare.* Washington, DC: U.S. Government Printing Office.

Congressional Budget Office. (1991). *Restructuring health insurance for medicare enrollees.* Washington, DC: U.S. Government Printing Office.

Congressional Budget Office. (1993a). *Economic implications of rising health care costs.* Washington, DC: U.S. Government Printing Office.

Congressional Budget Office. (1993b). *Trends in health spending: An update.* Washington, DC: U.S. Government Printing Office.

Congression Quarterly almanac (1960–2000). Washington, DC: Congressional Quarterly Press.

Conley, P. H. (2001). *Presidential mandates: How elections shape the national agenda.* Chicago: University of Chicago Press.

Converse, P. (1964). The Nature of Belief Systems in Mass Publics. In D. E. Apter (Ed.), *Ideology and Discontent.* New York: Free Press.

Converse, P. (1990). Popular Representation and the Distribution of Information. In J. Ferejohn and J. Kuklinski (Eds.), *Information and Democratic Processes,* (pp. 369–388). Chicago: University of Illinois Press.

Dao, J. (1999, August 24). Bradley vows he'll support racial unity. *The New York Times,* p. A17.

Delli-Carpini, M., & Keeter, S. (1996). *What American citizens know and why it matters.* New Haven, CT: Yale University Press.

Downs, A. (1957). *An economic theory of democracy.* New York: Harper & Row.

Downs, A. (1993). The origins of an economic theory of democracy. In B. Groffman (Ed.), *Information, participation, and choice,* pp. 198–201. Ann Arbor: University of Michigan Press.

Edelman, M. (1964). *The symbolic uses of politics.* Urbana: University of Illinois Press.

Edwards, G. C., III. (1983). *The public presidency: The pursuit of popular support.* New York: St. Martin's Press.

Edwards, G. C., III. (1989). *At the margins: Presidential leadership of congress.* New Haven, CT: Yale University Press.

Edwards, G. C., III. (1991). Presidential influence in Congress: If we ask the wrong questions, we get the wrong answers. *American Journal of Political Science, 35,* 724–729.

Edwards, G. C., III, Mitchell, W., & Welch, R. (1995). Explaining presidential approval: The significance of issue salience. *American Journal of Political Science, 39,* 108–134.

Erber, R., & Lau, R. (1990). Political cyniciam revisited: An information-processing reconciliation of policy-based and incumbency-based interpretations of changes in trust in government. *American Journal of Political Science, 34,* 236–253.

Erickson, R., Wright, G., & McIver, J. (1993). *Statehouse democracy: Public opinion and policy in the American states.* New York: Cambridge University Press.

Eyestone, R. (1978). *From social issues to public policy.* New York: Wiley.

Feldstein, P. J. (1993). *Health care economics* (4th ed.). Albany, NY: Delmar.

Fenno, R. (1978). *Homestyle: House members in their districts.* Boston: Little, Brown.

Ferejohn, J., & Kuklinski, J. (1990). *Information and the democratic process.* Urbana: University of Illinois Press.

Fett, P. (1992). Truth in advertising: The revelation of presidential legislative priorities. *Western Political Quarterly, 45,* 895–920.

Fett, P. (1994). Presidential legislative priorities and legislator's voting decisions: An exploratory analysis. *Journal of Politics, 56,* 502–512.

Fischhoff, B., Slovic, P., & Lichenstein, S. (1980). Knowing what you want: Measuring labile values. In T. Wallsten (Ed.), *Cognitive Processes in Choice and Decision Behavior.* Hillsdale, NJ: Erlbaum.

Fishbein, M., & Ajzen, I. (1975). *Belief, Attitude, Intention and Behavior: An Introduction to Theory and Research.* Los Angeles: Addison-Wesley.

Fiske, S. T., & Taylor, S. E. (1991). *Social cognition* New York: McGraw-Hill.

Frech, H. E., III. (1996). *Competition and monopoly in medical care.* Washington, DC: AEI Press.

Fried, A. (1988). Abortion politics as symbolic politics: An investigation into belief systems. *Social Science Quarterly, 69,* 137–154.

Friedrich, R. J. (1982). In defense of multiplicative terms in multiple regression equations. *American Journal of Political Science, 26,* 797–833.

Gallup, G., Jr. (1994). *The Gallup poll.* Princeton, NJ: Gallup.

Gallup, G., Jr. (1996). *The Gallup poll.* Princeton, NJ: Gallup.

Gallup, G., Jr. (2000). *The Gallup poll.* Princeton, NJ: Gallup.

Gallup, G., Jr. (2001). *The Gallup poll.* Princeton, NJ: Gallup.

Gilens, M. (1999). *Why Americans hate welfare: Race, media, and the politics of antipoverty policy.* Chicago: University of Chicago Press.

Gilens, M. (2000). Political ignorance and American democracy. Paper presented at the annual meeting of the Midwest Political Science Association, Chicago.

Gilens, M. (2001). Political ignorance and collective policy preferences. *American Political Science Review, 95*(2): 379–396.

Gooderis, J., & Hogan, A. (Eds.). (1994). *Improving access to health care: What can the states do?* Kalamazoo, MI: Upjohn Institute.

Government Accounting Office. (1991a). *Canadian health insurance: Lessons for the United States.* Washington, DC: U.S. Government Printing Office.

Government Accounting Office. (1991b). *Fraud and abuse: Stronger controls needed in federal employees health benefits program.* Washington, DC: U.S. Government Printing Office.

Government Accounting Office. (1992a). *Federal health benefits program: Analysis of contingency and special reserves.* Washington, DC: U.S. Government Printing Office.

Government Accounting Office. (1992b). *Federal employees health benefits program: Stronger controls needed to reduce administrative costs.* Washington, DC: U.S. Government Printing Office.

Government Accounting Office. (1992c). *Health care spending: Nonpolicy factors account for most state differences.* Washington, DC: U.S. Government Printing Office.

Graber, D. (2000). *Media power in politics.* Washington, DC: Congressional Quarterly Press.

Graig, L. (1999). *Health of nations* (3rd ed.). Washington, DC: Congressional Quarterly Press.

Granavetter, M. (1973). The strength of weak ties. *American Journal of Sociology, 78,* 1360–1380.

Granavetter, M. (1985). Economic action and social structure: The problem of embededness. *American Journal of Sociology, 91,* 481–510.

Greene, W. H. (1997). *Econometric analysis* (3rd ed.). Upper Saddle River, NJ: Prentice-Hall.

Gujarati, D. N. (1995). *Basic econometrics* (3rd ed.). New York: McGraw-Hill.

Hacker, J. S. (1997). *The road to nowhere: The genesis of President Clinton's plan for health security.* Princeton, NJ: Princeton University Press.

Hamilton, J. (1994). *Time series analysis.* Princeton, NJ: Princeton University Press.

Hansen, O., Blendon, R. J., Brodie, M., Ortmans, J., James, M., Norton, C., & Rosenblatt, T. (1996). Lawmakers' views on the failure of health reform: A survey of members of congress staff. *Journal of Health Politics, Policy, and Law, 21,* 137–151.

Hanushek E. A., & Jackson, J. (1977). *Statistical methods for social scientists.* New York: Wiley.

Hardin, R. (1982). *Collective action.* Baltimore: Johns Hopkins University Press.

Hartley, T., & Russett, B. (1992). Public opinion and the common defense: Who governs military spending in the United States? *American Political Science Review, 86,* 905–915.

Higgins, E. T., & King, G. (1981). Accessibility of social constructs; Information-processing consequences of individual and contextual variability. In N. Cantor &

J. Kihlstrom (Eds.), *Personality, cognition, and social interactions*. Hillsdale, NJ: Erlbaum.

Higgins, E. T., Bargh, J. A., & Lombardi, W. (1985). The nature of priming effects on categorization. *Journal of Experimental Psychology: Learning, Memory, and Cognition, 11*, 59–69.

Hilgartner, S., & Bosk, C. L. (1988). The rise and fall of social problems: A public arenas model. *American Journal of Sociology, 94*, 53–78.

Hinich M., & Munger, M. (1997). *Analytical politics*. New York: Cambridge University Press.

Huckfeldt, R., & Sprague, J. (1991). Discussant effects on vote choice: Intimacy, structure, and interdependence. *Journal of Politics, 53*(1), 122–158.

Huddy, L., Jones, J. M., & Chard, R. E. (2001). Compassionate politics: Self-Interest versus altruism in support for old-age programs. *Political Psychology, 22*(3), 443–471.

Ingram, H., & Schneider, A. (1995). Social construction (continued). *American Political Science Review, 89*(2), 441–446.

Iyengar, S. (1987). Television news and citizen's explanations of national affairs. *American Political Science Review, 81*, 815–831.

Iyengar, S. (1990). Shortcuts to political knowledge: The role of selective attention and accessibility. In J. Ferejohn & J. Kuklinski (Eds.), *Information and Democratic Processes* (pp. ___). Urban: University of Illinois Press.

Iyengar, S. (1991). *Is anyone responsible? How television frames political issues.* Chicago: University of Chicago Press.

Iyengar, S. (1993). *Who's responsible?* Chicago: University of Chicago Press.

Iyengar, S., & Kinder, D. R. (1987). *News that matters* Chicago: University of Chicago Press.

Iyengar, S., Peters, M. D., & Kinder, D. R. (1982). Experimental demonstrations of the "not-so-minimal" consequences of television news programs. *American Political Science Review, 76*(4), 848–858.

Iyengar, S., Peters, M. D., Kinder, D. R., & Krosnick, J. A. (1984). The evening news and presidential evaluations. *Journal of Personality and Social Psychology, 46*, 778–787.

Jacobs, L. (1993). *The health of nations: Public opinion and the making of American and British health policy.* New York: Cornell University Press.

Jacobs, L., & Shapiro, R. (1994). Questioning the conventional wisdom on public opinion on health reform. *PS: Political Science and Politics, 27*(2), 208–214.

Jacobs, L., & Shapiro, R. (2000). *Politicians don't pander: Political manipulation and the loss of democratic responsiveness.* Chicago: University of Chicago Press.

Jacobs, L. R., Shapiro, R. Y., & Schulman, E. C. (1993). The polls—poll trends: Medical care in the United States—An update. *Public Opinion Quarterly, 57*(3), 394–427.

Jacoby, W. G. (1988). The impact of party identification on issue attitudes. *American Journal of Political Science, 32*(3), 643–661.

Jacoby, W. (1991). Ideological identification and issue attitudes. *American Journal of Political Science, 35,* 178–205.

Jamieson, K. H. (1998). The role of the press in the health care reform debate of 1993–1994. In D. Graber, D. McQuail, & P. Norris (Eds.), *Politics of news, news of politics* (pp. 110–131). Washington, DC: Congressional Quarterly Press.

Jenkins-Smith, H., & Sabatier, P. (1993). *Policy change and learning: An advocacy coalition approach.* San Francisco: Westview Press.

Johnson, L. (1964). *The Public Papers of the Presidents of the United States: 1932 to 1994.* Washington, DC: U.S. Government Printing Office.

Jones, B. (1995). *Reconceiving decision-making in democratic politics: Attention, choice, and public policy.* Chicago: University of Chicago Press.

Kahneman, D., & Tversky, A. (1979). Prospect theory: An analysis of decision under risk. *Econometrica, 47,* 263–291.

Kahneman, D., & Tversky, A. (1982). The psychology of preferences. *Science, 246,* 136–142.

Kahneman, D., & Tversky, A. (1984). Choices, values, and frames. *American Psychologist, 39,* 341–350.

Kelley, S. (1956). *Profession public relations and political power,* Baltimore: Johns Hopkins Press.

Kenny, C. (1994). The microenvironment of attitude change. *Journal of Politics, 56,* 715–728.

Kernell, S. (1986). *Going public: New strategies of presidential leadership* (2nd ed.). Washington, DC: Congressional Quarterly Press.

Kernell, S. (1993). *Going public: New strategies of presidential leadership,* (2nd ed.). Washington, DC: Congressional Quarterly Press.

Kinder, D. R., & Sears, D. (1985). Public opinion and political action. In *Handbook of Social Psychology,* 705–714.

King, G. (1993). *Unifying political methodology: The likelihood theory of statistical inference.* New York: Cambridge University Press.

Kingdon, J. (1984). *Agendas, alternatives, and public policies.* Boston: Little, Brown.

Kingdon, J. (1989). *Congressmen's voting decisions.* Ann Arbor: University of Michigan Press.

Koff, T. H., & Park, R. W. (1993) *Aging public policy: Bonding the generations.* Amityville, NY: Baywood.

Koff, T. H., & Park, R. W. (1999). *Aging public policy: Bonding the generations* (2nd ed.). Amityville, NY: Baywood.

Krosnick, J. A., & Kinder, D. R. (1990). Altering the foundations of support for the president through priming. *American Political Science Review, 84*, 497–512.

Kuklinski, J. H., & Hurley, N. L. (1994). On hearing and interpreting the political messages: A cautionary tale of cue-taking. *Journal of Politics, 56*, 729–751.

Kuklinski, J., Metlay, D., & Kay, W. D. (1982). Citizen knowledge and choices on the complex issue of nuclear power. *American Journal of Political Science, 26*, 620–641.

Kuklinski, J., Quirk, P., Schwieder, D., & Rich, R. (1996). *Misinformation and public opinion.* Paper presented at the annual meeting of the Midwest Political Science Association, Chicago.

Kunda, Z. (1990). The case for motivated reasoning. *Psychological Bulletin, 108*, 480–498.

Lancaster, K. (1966). A new approach to consumer theory. *Journal of Political Economy, 74*, 101–121.

Lasswell, H. (1963). *Who gets what, when and how?* New York: McGraw-Hill.

Lazarsfeld, P., Berelson, B., & Gaudet, H. (1954). *The people's choice.* New York: Columbia University Press.

Levit, K., Lazenby, H., & Sivarajan, L. (1996). Health care spending in 1994: Slowest in decades. *Health Affairs, 15*, 130–144.

Lindeman, M. (1996). *Studying informed preferences: Measures, models, and mysteries.* Paper presented at the annual meeting of the Midwest Political Science Association, Chicago.

Lindeman, M. (1997). *Public preferences in health care: Evidence from deliberative studies.* Paper presented at the annual meeting of the Midwest Political Science Association, Chicago.

Lippman, W. (1965) *Public opinion.* New York: Free Press. (Original work published 1922)

Liska, A. (1984). A critical examination of the causal structure of the Fishbein/Ajzen attitude-behavior mode. *Social Psychology Quarterly, 47*, 61–74.

Lodge, M, McGraw, K., & Stroh, P. (1989). An impression-driven model of candidate evaluation. *American Political Science Review, 83*, 399–419.

Lombardi, W. J., Higgins, E. T., & Bargh, J. A. (1987). The role of consciousness in priming effects on categorization: Assimilation versus contrast as a function of awareness of the priming task. *Personality and Social Psychology Bulletin, 13*, 411–429.

Long, J. S. (1997). *Regression models for categorical and limited dependent variables.* Thousand Oaks, CA: Sage.

Lupia, A. (1994). Short cuts versus encyclopedias: Information and voting behavior in California insurance reform election. *American Political Science Review, 88,* 63–76.

Lynch, T. (1995). *Public budgeting in America* (4th ed.). Englewood Cliffs, NJ: Prentice-Hall.

MacKuen, M. B. (1983). Political drama, economic conditions and the dynamics of presidential popularity. *American Journal of Political Science, 27,* 165–192.

Maddala, G. S. (1983). *Limited dependent and qualitative variables in econometrics.* Cambridge: Cambridge University Press.

Marmor, T. R. (1994). *Understanding health care reform.* New Haven, CT: Yale University Press.

Mayer, R. N. (1991). Gone yesterday, Here today: Consumer issues in the agenda-setting process. *Journal of Social Issues, 47,* 21–39.

Mayhew, D. R. (1974). *Congress: The electoral connection.* New Haven, CT: Yale University Press.

Mayhew, D. R. (1991). *Divided we govern: Party control, lawmaking, and investigations 1946–1990.* New Haven, CT: Yale University Press.

Mazmanian, D. A., & Sabatier, P. A. (1980). A multivariate model of public policy-making. *American Journal of Political Science, 24*(3), 439–468.

McCarthy, J. D., McPhail, C., Smith, J. (1996). Images of protest: Dimensions of selection bias in media coverage of Washington demonstrations, 1982 and 1991. *American Sociological Review, 61,* 478–499.

McClosky, H., & Zaller, J. (1984). *The American ethos: Public attitudes toward capitalism and democracy.* Cambridge: Harvard University Press.

McCombs, M., & Shaw, D. (1972). The agenda-setting function of mass media. *Public Opinion Quarterly, 36,* 176–187.

McCullough, D. (1992). *Truman.* New York: Simon & Schuster.

McDermott, M. (1997). Voting cues in low-information elections: Candidate gender as a social information variable in contemporary United States elections. *American Journal of Political Science, 41,* 270–283.

McFarland, A. S. (1987). Interest groups and theories of power in America. *British Journal of Political Science, 17*(1), 129–147.

McFarland, A. S. (1991). Interest groups and political time: Cycles in America. *British Journal of Political Science, 21*(2), 257–284.

McGraw, K. M., & Ling, C. (2002). Media priming of presidential and group evaluations. *Political Communication.*

Meyer, J. E. (1994). HCFA review a warning about life under a single payer. *American Medical News, 37,* 16.

Miller, A., Wattenberg, M., & Malanchuk, O. (1986). Schematic assessment of presidential candidates. *American Political Science Review, 80,* 521–540.

Mondak, J. (1993). Sources, cues, and policy approval: The cognitive dynamics of public support for the Reagan agenda. *American Journal of Political Science, 37,* 186–212.

Mondak, J. (1999). Reconsidering the measurement of political knowledge. *Political Anlayis, 8,* 57–81.

Morrow, J. (1994). *Game theory for political scientists.* Princeton, NJ: Princeton University Press.

Mueller, J. E. (1970). Presidential popularity from Truman to Johnson. *American Political Science Review, 64,* 18–34.

Mueller, J. E. (1973). *War, presidents and public opinion.* New York: Wiley.

Mutz, D. C. (1993). Direct and indirect routes to politicizing personal experience: Does knowledge make a difference? *Public Opinion Quarterly, 57*(4), 483–502.

National Institutes of Health. (2001). *NIH almanac.* Washington, DC: U.S. Government Printing Office.

Nelson, R. R., & Winter, S. G. (1982). The Schumpeterian tradeoff revisited. *American Economic Review, 72*(1), 114–132.

Nelson, R. R., & Winter, S. G. (1985). *Evolutionary theory of economic change.* Cambridge: Harvard University Press.

Neuman, W. R., Just, M. R., & Crigler, A. N. (1992). *Common knowledge and the construction of political meaning.* Chicago: University of Chicago Press.

Neustadt, R. E. (1990). *Presidential power and the modern presidents: The politics of leadership from Roosevelt to Reagan.* New York: Free Press.

North, D. (1990). *Institutions, institutional change, and economic performance.* New York: Cambridge University Press.

Norpoth, H. (1987). Guns and butter and government popularity in Britain. *American Political Science Review, 81*(3), 949–959.

Olson, M. (1965). *The logic of collective action.* Cambridge: Harvard University Press.

Ostrom, C. W. (1990). *Time series analysis: Regression techniques* (2nd edition). Newbury Park, CA: Sage.

Ostrom, C. W., Jr., & Simon, D. M. (1985). Promise and performance: A dynamic model of presidential popularity. *American Political Science Review, 79,* 334–358.

Ostrom, C. W., Jr., & Simon, D. M. (1988). The president's public. *American Journal of Political Science, 32,* 1096–1119.

Ostrom, C. W., Jr., & Simon, D. M. (1989). The man in the teflon suit: The environmental connection, political drama, and popular support in the Reagan presidency. *Public Opinion Quarterly, 53,* 353–387.

Ostrum, A., & Iacobucci, D. (1995). Consumer trade-offs and the evaluation of services. *Journal of Marketing, 59,* 17–28.

Overman, E. S., & Cahill, A. G. (1994). Information, market government, and health policy: A study of health data organizations in the states. *Journal of Policy Analysis and Management, 13,* 435–453.

Page, B. I., & Shapiro, R. Y. (1983). Effects of public opinion on policy. *American Political Science Review, 77,* 175–190.

Page, B. I., & Shapiro, R. Y. (1984). Presidents as policy leaders: Some new evidence. *Policy Studies Journal, 12,* 649–661.

Page, B. I., & Shapiro, R. Y. (1992). *The rational public: Fifty years of trends in Americans' policy preferences.* Chicago: University of Chicago Press.

Page, B., Shapiro, R., & Dempsey, G. (1987). What moves public opinion? *American Political Science Review, 81,* 23–24.

Parker, S. L. (1995). Toward an understanding of rally effects: Public opinion in the Persian Gulf war. *Public Opinion Quarterly, 59,* 526–546.

Penzer, J. Ross. (1995). Grading the report card: Lessons from cognitive psychology, marketing, and the law of information disclosure for quality assessment in health care reform. *Yale Journal of Regulation, 12,* 207–256.

Peterson, M. Alex. (1990). *Legislating together: The White House and Capitol Hill from Eisenhower to Reagan.* Cambridge: Harvard University Press.

Peterson, M. Alex. (1994). Health care and the Hill: Why is this year different from all others? *PS: Political Science and Politics, 27*(2), 202–207.

Petty, R. E., & Cacioppo, J. T. (1986). *Communication and persuasion: Central and peripheral routes to attitude change.* New York: Springer-Verlag.

Polsby, N. (1984). *Political innovations in America: The politics of policy initiation.* New Haven, CT: Yale University Press.

Popkin, S. (1991). *The reasoning voter: Communication and persuasion in presidential campaigns.* Chicago: University of Chicago Press.

Price, V. & Zaller, J. (1993). Who gets the news: Alternative measures of news reception and their implications of research. *Public Opinion Quartarly, 57,* 133–164.

The Public Papers of the Presidents of the United States: 1932 to 1994. Washington, DC: U.S. Government Printing Office.

Quattrone, G. A., & Tversky, A. (1984). Causal versus diagnostic contingencies: On self-deception and voters' illusion. *Journal of Personality and Social Psychology, 46,* 237–248.

Quattrone, G. A., & Tversky, A. (1988). Contrasting rational and psychological analyses of political choice. *American Political Science Review, 82*, 719–736.

Ragsdale, L. (1984). The politics of presidential speechmaking, 1949–1980. *American Political Science Review, 78*, 971–984.

Ragsdale, L. (1987). Presidential speechmaking and the public audience: Individual presidents and group attitudes. *Journal of Politics, 49*, 704–736.

Rahn, W., Aldrich, J., & Borgida, E. (1994). Individual and contextual variations in political candidate appraisal. *American Political Science Review, 88*, 193–199.

Riker, W. H. (1986). *The art of political manipulation*. New Haven, CT: Yale University Press.

Rivers, D., & Rose, N. L. (1985). Passing the president's program: Public opinion and presidential influence in Congress. *American Journal of Political Science, 29*, 183–196.

Rivers, D., & Vuong, Q. H. (1988). Limited information estimators and exogeneity tests for simultaneous probit models. *Journal of Econometrics, 39*, 347–366.

Roberts, N. C., & King, P. J. (1996). *Transforming public policy: dynamics of policy entrepreneurship and innovation*. San Francisco: Jossey-Bass.

Rosen, C. M., (1973). A test of presidential leadership of public opinion: The split ballot technique. *Polity, 6*, 282–290.

Schiller, W. J. (1995). Senators as political entrepreneurs: Using bill sponsorship to shape legislative agendas. *American Journal of Political Science, 39*, 186–203.

Schlesinger, M., & Lau, R. (2000). The meaning and measure of policy metaphors. *American Political Science Review, 93*(3), 611–626.

Schneider, A., & Ingram, H. (1990). Behavioral assumptions of policy tools. *Journal of Politics, 52*(2), 510–529.

Schneider, A., & Ingram, H. (1993). Social constructions and target populations: Implications for politics and policy. *American Political Science Review, 87*(2), 334–347.

Schneider, M., & Teske, P. (1992). Toward a theory of the political entrepreneur: Evidence from Local Government. *American Political Science Review, 86*(3), 737–747.

Schneider, M., & Teske, P. (1993). The antigrowth entrepreneur: Challenging the "equilibrium" of the growth machine. *Journal of Politics, 55*(3), 720–736.

Schneider, M., & Teske P. (with Mintrom, M.). (1995). *Public entrepreneurs: agents for change in American government*. Princeton, NJ: Princeton University Press.

Schoemaker, P. (1993). Determinants of risk-taking: Behavioral and economic views. *Journal of Risk and Uncertainty, 6*, 49–73.

Schottland, C. I. (1963). *The Social Security program in the United States*. New York: Appleton Century Crofts.

Sears, D., Lau, R., Tyler, T., & Allen, H. (1980). Self-interest vs. symbolic politics in policy attitudes and presidential voting. *American Political Science Review, 74,* 670–684.

Sigelman, L. (1980). Gauging the public responses to presidential leadership. *Presidential Studies Quarterly, 10,* 427–433.

Sigelman, L., & Sigelman, C. K. (1981). Presidential leadership of public opinion: From benevolent leader to kiss of death. *Experimental Study of Politics, 7,* 1–22.

Simon, H. A. (1947). *Administrative behavior*. New York: Free Press.

Simon, H. A. (1955). A behavioral model of rational choice. *Quarterly Journal of Economics, 69,* 99–118.

Simon, H. A. (1956). Rational choice and the structure of the environment. *Psychological Review, 63,* 129–138.

Simon, H. A. (1979). *Models of thought*. New Haven, CT: Yale University Press.

Simon, H. A. (1985). Human nature in politics: the dialogue of psychology with political science. *American Political Science Review, 79,* 293–304.

Simon, H. A. (1991). Black ravens and a white shoe. *British Journal of Philosophy of Science, 42,* 339–342.

Skocpol, T. (1993). Is the time finally ripe? health insurance reforms in the 1990s. *Journal of Health Politics, Policy, and Law, 18,* 275–292.

Skocpol, T. (1995). *Social policy in the United States: Future possibilities in historical perspective*. Princeton, NJ: Princeton University Press.

Slade, S. (1994). *Goal based decision making*. Hillsdale, NJ: Earlbaum.

Smith, E. R. A. N. (1989). *The unchanging American voter*. Berkeley and Los Angeles: University of California Press.

Smith, J. A. (1991). *The idea brokers: Think tanks and the rise of the new policy elite*. New York: Free Press.

Staggenborg, S. (1987). Life-style preferences and social movement recruitment: Abortion conflict . *Social Science Quarterly, 68,* 779–797.

Stanley, H. W., & Niemi, R. G. (1995). *Vital statistics on American politics: Fifth edition*. Washington, DC: Congressional Quarterly Press.

Starr, P. (1982). *The social transformation of American medicine*. New York: Basic Books.

Stimson, J. A. (1999). *Public opinion in America: Moods, cycles, & swings* (2nd ed.). San Francisco: Westview Press.

Stimson, J A., MacKuen. M. B., & Erikson, R. S. (1995). Dynamic representation. *American Political Science Review, 89*, 543–565.

Stone, W., Rapoport, R., & Atkeson, L. (1995). A simulation model of presidential choice. *American Journal of Political Science, 39*, 135–161.

Sullivan, T. (1991a). The bank account presidency: A new measure and evidence on the temporal path of presidential influence. *American Journal of Political Science, 35*, 686–723.

Sullivan, T. (1991b). Wrong questions, 0-questions, legitimate questions, reasoned answers: Affirming the study of temporal path. *American Journal of Political Science, 35*, 730–737.

Teske, P., Schneider, M., Mintrom, M., & Best. S. (1993). Establishing the micro foundations of a macro theory: Information, movers, and the competitive local market for public goods. *American Political Science Review, 87*, 702–713.

Thomas, D. B., & Bass, L. (1982). Presidential identification and mass-public compliance with official policy: The case of the carter energy program. *Policy Studies Journal, 10*, 448–464.

Thomas, D. B., & Sigelman, L. (1985). Presidential identification and policy leadership: Experimental evidence on the Reagan case. In G. C. Edwards, III, S. Shull, N. C. Thomas (Eds.), *The presidency and public policy making*. Pittsburgh, PA: University of Pittsburgh Press.

Truman, D. (1951). *The governmental process*. New York: Knopf.

Turner, C. F., & Kraus, E. (1978). Fallible indicators of the subjective state of the nation. *American Psychologist, 33*, 456–470.

Tversky, A. (1972). Elimination by aspects: A theory of choice. *Psychological Review, 79*, 281–299.

Tversky, A., & Kahneman, D. (1974). Judgment under uncertainty: Heuristics and biases. *Science, 185*, 1124–1131.

Verba, S., Scholzman, K., & Brady, H. (1996). *Voice and equality: Civic voluntarism in American politics*. Cambridge: Harvard University Press.

Viscusi, W. K., & Evans, W. N. (1990). Utility functions that depend on health status: Estimates and economic implications. *American Economic Review, 80*(3), 353–374.

Weissert, C. & Weissert, W. (1996). *Governing health: The politics of health policy*. Baltimore: Johns Hopkins University Press.

West, D. M., Heith, D., & Goodwin, C. (1996). Harry and Louise go to Washington: Political advertising and health care reform. *Journal of Health Politics, Policy, and Law, 21*, 35–68.

White House Domestic Policy Council, The. (1993). *Health security: The president's report to the American people.* Washington, DC: U.S. Government Printing Office.

Wildavsky, A. (1988). The new politics of the budgetary process. New York: Scott Foresman.

Wilsford, D. (1994). Path dependency, or why history makes it difficult but not impossible to reform health care systems in a big way. *Journal of Public Policy, 14,* 251–283.

Wright, G. C., Rieselbach, L. N., & Dodd, L. (1986). *Congress and policy change.* Edison, NJ: Agathon Press.

Wyer, R. S., & Srull, T. K. (1984). Category accessibility: Some theoretic and empirical issues concerning the processing of social stimulus information. In E. T. Higgins, N. A. Kuiper, & M. P. Zanna (Eds.), *Social cognition: The Ontario symposium.* Hillsdale, NJ: Erlbaum.

Yankelovich, D. (1995). The debate that wasn't: The public and the Clinton plan. *Health Affairs, 14,* 7–23.

Zaller, J. (1986). The effects of political involvement on Public attitudes and Voting Behaior. Paper present at the annual meeting of the American Political Science Association.

Zaller, J. (1992). *The nature and origins of mass opinion.* Cambridge: Cambridge University Press.

Zaller, J., & Feldman, S. (1992). A simple theory of survey response: Answering questions versus revealing preferences. *American Journal of Political Science, 36,* 579–616.

Index

·

Mayhew, David, 60, 62, 65, 68, 144
Mazmanian, Daniel, 68
McCain, John, 118
McCarthy, John, 56, 62
McClosky, Herbert, 24, 55
McCullough, David, 59, 62
McDermott, Monika, 80
McFarland, Andrew, 24
McGraw, Kathleen, 94, 95
McIver, John, 76, 94, 129
McPhail, Clark, 56, 62
McPhee, William, 84
media exposure, 96
media priming, 94, 95, 96, 102, 107, 109,
110, 111, 112, 113, 115, 116, 117, 118,
119, 120, 122, 123
Medicaid, 7, 8, 12, 17, 19, 21, 33, 37, 39,
42, 45, 53, 60, 63, 66, 69, 70, 73, 75,
109, 126, 128, 137, 153, 154, 155
(chapter 1) n 1
Medicare, 7, 8, 12, 17, 19, 21, 33, 37, 39,
42, 45, 53, 60, 63, 66, 69, 70, 73, 75,
109, 126, 128, 134, 137, 153, 154, 155
(chapter 1) n 1
Metlay, Daniel, 76, 78
Miller, Arthur, 79
Mintrom, Michael, 13, 22, 50, 51, 52, 62
Mitchell, George, 98
Mithchells, William, 57
Mondak, Jeffrey, 78, 79, 80
Mueller, John, 56
Munger, Michael, 14, 157 (chapter 5) n4
Mutz, Diana, 77

Nagler, Jonathan, 157 (chapter 5) n4
National Council of Senior Citizens, 35
National Election Study (NES), 79, 102,
112
national health insurance in the U.S., 17
National Institutes of Health (NIH), 16
Nelson, Richard, 24
Neuman, W. Russell, 94, 148, 150
Neustadt, Richard, 48, 56, 130
New Deal, 22, 59, 110
New Hampshire Primary, 158 (chapter
7) n3

North American Free Trade Agreement
(NAFTA), 72
North, Douglass, 11, 12, 13, 14, 16, 17,
21, 22, 23, 24, 25, 35, 36, 43, 49, 52,
91, 93, 94, 95, 107, 126, 127
Northpoth, Helmut, 137

occam's razor, 125
Oregon and section 1115 waivers, 19
Ostrom, Charles, 38, 138

Page, Benjamin, 15, 38, 41, 55, 58, 59,
67, 76, 77, 94, 134
Park, Richard, 33, 34, 35, 38, 45, 58,
129
Path Dependence, 7, 11, 12, 16, 21, 23,
29, 36, 38, 39, 76, 91, 107, 113, 126,
127, 128, 129
Perkins, Frances, 16, 58
Perot, Ross, 85
Peters, Mark, 115, 153
Peterson, Mark, 53, 66, 72, 82
Petty, Richard, 83
Pika, Joseph, 63
policy change, 36, 49, 52, 91, 93, 125,
127, 128, 131, 133
policy entrepreneur, 25, 26, 49, 50, 51
policy metaphors, 31, 32, 34, 35, 43, 46,
76, 96, 97, 102, 105
policy networks, 50
policy sophistication, 77, 78, 79, 80, 84,
94, 101, 102, 104, 105, 106, 107, 127
Polsby, Nelson, 25
Popkin, Samuel, 83
presidential mandate, 52, 53, 68, 72
presidential popularity, 57, 63, 68, 72
presidents and agenda-setting, 49
public mood, 29, 38, 41, 42, 44, 45, 55,
129
public opinion, 49, 75, 83, 90
punctuated equilibrium, 6, 7

Ragsdale, Lynne, 57
Rahn, Wendy, 79
Rapoport, Ronald, 79
Reagan, Ronald, 58, 70, 78, 112

DATE DUE

Demco, Inc. 38-293